What happened in the Scottsboro case wasn't unusual. What was unusual was that the world heard about it.

—Haywood Patterson

LS OF THE SCOTTSBORO BOYS:
LIES, PREJUDICE, AND
FOURTEENTH AMENDMENT

RY DANE BRIMNER

ACCUSED!

CALKINS CREEK
AN IMPRINT OF HIGHLIGHTS
Honesdale, Pennsylvania

*For Sneed B. Collard III, steadfast friend
and unwavering champion for justice and equality.*

All persons born or naturalized in the United States, and subject to the jurisdiction thereof, are citizens of the United States and of the State wherein they reside. No State shall make or enforce any law which shall abridge the privileges or immunities of citizens of the United States; nor shall any State deprive any person of life, liberty, or property, without due process of law; nor deny to any person within its jurisdiction the equal protection of the law.

—US Constitution,
Fourteenth Amendment,
Section 1

For information about permission to reproduce selections from this book, please contact permissions@highlights.com.

Calkins Creek
An Imprint of Highlights
815 Church Street
Honesdale, Pennsylvania 18431
calkinscreekbooks.com
Printed in China

ISBN: 978-1-62979-775-5 (hardcover)
ISBN: 978-1-68437-894-4 (eBook)

Library of Congress Control Number: 2019936024

First edition
10 9 8 7 6 5 4 3 2 1

Design by Barbara Grzeslo
The text is set in Garamond 3.
The titles are set in Impact.

CONTENTS

Who Were the

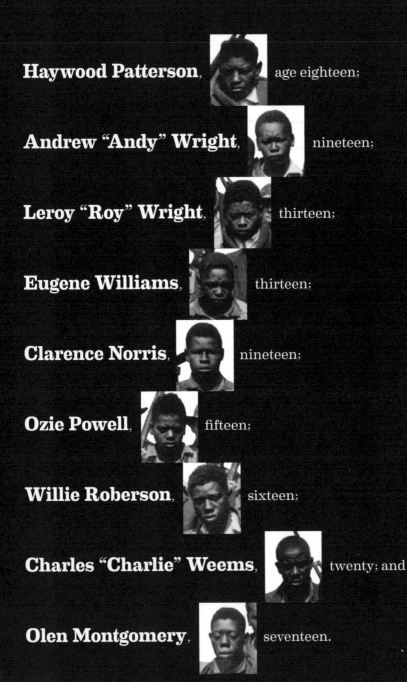

Haywood Patterson, age eighteen;

Andrew "Andy" Wright, nineteen;

Leroy "Roy" Wright, thirteen;

Eugene Williams, thirteen;

Clarence Norris, nineteen;

Ozie Powell, fifteen;

Willie Roberson, sixteen;

Charles "Charlie" Weems, twenty; and

Olen Montgomery, seventeen.

Scottsboro Boys?

With the exception of Roberson and Montgomery, the young men "were riding the freight for the same reason, to go somewhere and find work," recalled Patterson. Roberson had been on his way to Memphis, Tennessee, to be treated for two sexually transmitted diseases, gonorrhea and syphilis; he was so disabled by these ailments that he could barely walk. Montgomery, who was nearly blind, was also bound for Memphis, on his way to see what doctors could do about his vision.

JOURNEY INTERRUPTED

A posse of deputized white farmers carrying pistols and shotguns rousted Haywood Patterson and eight other young black men from the forty-two–car Alabama Great Southern Railroad freight train as it rolled to a stop in Paint Rock, Alabama. It was Wednesday, March 25, 1931, at around two o'clock in the afternoon.

Except for Patterson and his three Chattanooga, Tennessee, friends—Eugene Williams and brothers Andy and Roy Wright—the nine black youths were relative strangers. They had been riding in different railcars, and some of them met for the first time when a scuffle broke out with several young white fellows who also were "stealing a ride." As Patterson explained, the fight started "with a white foot on my black hand," which almost knocked Patterson off the oil tanker he was riding on. The young white men wanted the Memphis-bound train to themselves. Almost all of them, blacks and whites, were "hoboing from one place to another looking for work." The desperation of the Great Depression had driven them from their homes to find a way to provide for themselves, with perhaps a little something left over to send back to their families. But during the tussle, the black men got the upper hand. "Some of them [the white boys] jumped off [the slow-moving train]," said Patterson, "and some we put off."

Fearing a lynching in Scottsboro, Governor Benjamin Meeks Miller called out the Alabama National Guard to protect the nine black youths. They are, from left, Clarence Norris, Olen Montgomery,

Andy Wright, Willie Roberson, Ozie Powell, Eugene Williams, Charlie Weems, Roy Wright, and Haywood Patterson.

Angered and embarrassed at losing the fight, the white boys made their way to Stevenson, Alabama, the closest town through which the freight train had passed, and lodged a complaint at the depot. The stationmaster there called ahead to Scottsboro, Alabama, to report the violence that had occurred and to have the black youths rounded up, but the train had already passed through the town. Jackson County sheriff M. L. Wann called Deputy Sheriff Charlie Latham in Paint Rock, the next stop, and told him to deputize as many men as he needed to "capture every negro on the train and bring them to Scottsboro."

Now, in Paint Rock, Latham and the farmers roped the "Negroes together." They took down everyone's name and forced all nine into the back of a truck. "Some had not even been in the fight on the train," Patterson recalled later. "A few in the fight got away so the posse [of farmers] never picked them up."

Patterson asked a man what the fuss was about.

"Assault and attempt to murder," the man answered.

Along with the black youths, a young white man and "two girls dressed in men's overalls" were taken from the railcars. It was then Patterson first realized that women also had been hoboing aboard the Alabama Great Southern Railroad.

The truck, loaded with its cargo of youthful hoboes, made the short, dusty journey from Paint Rock to Scottsboro, the seat of Jackson County. Here, the boys were taken to the two-story jail, where they were placed in a cell with "flat bars, checkerboard style, around the windows."

The black youths were hot, sweaty, and scared. Outside the window of their cell, they could see a crowd of excited, noisy white folks beginning to gather. Patterson described them as "mad ants, white ants, sore that somebody had stepped on their hill." Some of the younger boys started to cry.

As the afternoon wore on, the horde of several hundred grew louder and angrier and began calling for Sheriff Wann to bring the boys outside. They had one thought on their minds: vigilante justice, or lynching. Wann ordered the people to go home, but they were in no mood to listen. They threatened to rush the jail and take the youths by force. When they started toward the door, the sheriff pulled his gun. "If you come in here," he said, "I will blow your brains out. Get away from here."

As the hours passed and night fell upon Scottsboro, Sheriff Wann turned off the lights inside the jail. He realized that although the crowd outside had become smaller, its anger had not diminished. He became convinced he needed help to keep the townsfolk from storming the jail. He placed a telephone call to Governor Benjamin Meeks Miller and requested National Guard troops to safeguard his prisoners. Miller, who had taken a firm stand against mob justice and lynching throughout his political career, ordered troops to Scottsboro from their headquarters twenty miles away, and by eleven o'clock that night armed Guardsmen were on their way.

Patterson and the others had been locked up for hours before they learned what the excitement outside the jailhouse was really about. On Thursday morning, Wann took the youths out of their cell and lined them up in the hall. He brought in two women, "the two gals dressed like men rounded up at Paint Rock." According to Clarence Norris, one of the boys in the lineup, the sheriff said, "Miss Price, which one . . . had you?"

She went down the line, pointing at each one, "until she had picked out six," including Norris.

The sheriff asked Ruby Bates, the other woman, the same question, but she didn't speak.

A guard spoke up for her: "Well, if those six had Miss Price it stands to reason the others had Miss Bates."

The Starnes Brigade of the Alabama National Guard answered the governor's emergency call to send troops to Scottsboro to protect the black youths accused of assaulting two white girls. The brigade was under the command of Major Joe Starnes.

seen center front, seventh from either left or right. He expected to

As Roy Wright recalled, however, the two women were twice brought into the jail where he and the eight others were being held and did not identify anyone as their attackers. It wasn't until they were brought in a third time that Thursday morning that Price identified six of the youths as having attacked her.

The black youths all denied the charge. They claimed they'd never seen the girls until they were pulled from the train in Paint Rock. Norris blurted out that the women were liars. When he did, a guard struck out with his bayonet, slicing Norris's "right hand open to the bone."

"You know damn well how to talk about white women," the guard screamed.

Norris knew all right. He also "knew if a white woman accused a black man of rape, he was as good as dead."

2

ACCUSED

Rape. There was hardly a more serious crime in the South than the rape of a white woman by a black man. This image had long fueled the Ku Klux Klan's stereotype of blacks as depraved and lay at the heart of segregation, the purpose of which was to keep white women safe by racial separation. Most black men understood that raping a white woman almost certainly guaranteed the hangman's noose. On reflection, Haywood Patterson said, "Only a Negro who is a fool or a crazy man . . . would chance his life for anything like that. A Negro with sound judgment and common sense is not going to do it. They [white people] are going to take his life away from him if he does. Every Negro man in the South knows that. No, most Negroes run away from that sort of thing, fear in their hearts." He also knew that a white woman's word against that of a black man was sufficient for conviction, assuming the man ever made it to trial.

It isn't clear who first made the accusation against the young men, twenty-three-year-old Victoria Price or seventeen-year-old Ruby Bates. A traveling salesman who was in Paint Rock that day said it was Bates who approached Deputy Sheriff Latham and told him that she and Price had been attacked by the nine black youths. Other witnesses claim that neither woman said anything about an assault until the deputy asked repeatedly whether the Negroes in the truck

America's First Terrorist Organization

Within months after the end of the Civil War in 1865, a small group of former Confederate soldiers gathered around a fireplace in the little Tennessee town of Pulaski, near the Alabama border. Bored, they decided to form a social club. As plans for the club evolved, they determined that, to heighten its mystery, it would be a secret organization, and the titles for the various offices would be as outrageous as possible. The head of this secret society would be known as the Grand Cyclops, after the one-eyed giant from Greek mythology. Other positions included a Grand Magi, Grand Turk, and Grand Scribe. When they found others to join them, they called the new members Ghouls.

The men wanted a name for their society that was unusual and fitting for a group headed by a Grand Cyclops. One of the Confederate veterans turned to the Greek language and suggested *kuklos*, or circle. Another added the word *clan* because he liked the hard sound of the two words—*kuklos* and *clan*—together. Eventually, they settled on Ku Klux Klan. Soon after establishing the society's official name, the men disguised themselves in sheets, grotesque masks, and pointed hats, and rode their horses through the streets of Pulaski. It didn't take them long to realize that their antics produced a chilling effect among poor, uneducated people, some of whom believed the night riders were the ghosts of Confederate dead.

By early 1866, word of the Klan had crossed state borders, and membership had grown. The silliness behind the first night rides had turned to hate, as violence and fear became a means to keep African Americans from enjoying the rights and freedoms won with the Civil War. According to civil rights activist Julian Bond, the secret "society was America's first terrorist organization."

had bothered them. Either way, the women's claim that they had been raped didn't come until some time after the train had stopped and all the hoboes had been rounded up.

It didn't take long that Wednesday afternoon for news of the alleged assault to spread like wildfire among the posse of farmers in Paint Rock, many of whom believed there was no swifter justice for a black man than to hang him from the end of a rope. Even so, the nine youths who were forced into the back of the truck weren't aware of what the two women had told the deputy sheriff or even that they had spoken to him. As for Latham, he had been ordered to bring the boys to Scottsboro, and he was determined to do it. He calmed the deputized farmers and told them to go home. The men were "orderly, though it would have taken just a little leading for a wholesale lynching."

About an hour after the young men were taken from Paint Rock, they sat in the Scottsboro jail, waiting. Sheriff Wann sent the women to two local physicians for examinations after learning about the rape allegations. Since the sheriff made no attempt to keep the women's assertions private, news of their accusations circulated through the town and into the hills beyond. Each retelling of the alleged attack grew more vivid and gruesome. By dusk, two to three hundred angry white people had gathered in town. They arrived by automobiles and, in a few cases, astride mules. Some of the farmers and mountain folk, most chewing tobacco and clad in worn, faded overalls, brought their wives and small children with them. It was the men who jostled to the front to have a better view of the jail.

Described by newspapers as unemployed cotton-mill workers and the daughters of two poor, Huntsville, Alabama, widows, Bates and Price told their tale to reporters and anybody else who would listen. They were being held as witnesses in another part of what Patterson called Scottsboro's "jimcrow jail." Jim Crow was the name given to the segregation practices of the South—whites here, blacks there.

Price dominated the jailhouse interviews, while Bates remained silent and still, except when she spit a stream of tobacco juice into a spittoon from time to time. By late Thursday afternoon, the local newspaper carried their story with a sensational headline:

NINE NEGRO MEN RAPE TWO WHITE GIRLS,
CHARGED

The women's hometown paper, the *Huntsville Daily Times*, printed a headline that read:

REVOLTING IN LAST DEGREE IN STORY OF GIRLS
Each Criminally Attacked by Six Negroes

The accompanying article went on to describe the crime as

"one of the most horrible ever perpetrated in the United States." It labeled the youths as "nine negro fiends who Wednesday criminally assaulted two Huntsville girls on a coal car." The young men's guilt was assumed by the press and by the white folks of Jackson County. Scottsboro's *Progressive Age* found "the details of the crime coming form [*sic*] the lips of two girls, Victoria Price and Ruby Bates . . . too revolting to be printed." But the *Jackson County Sentinel* wasn't as troubled. "While some of the negroes held the two white girls," it reported, "others of the fiends raped them, holding knives at their throats and beating them when they struggled."

Price and Bates said they had gone to Chattanooga to look for work. Their previous jobs in Huntsville had ended when falling cotton prices had forced the mills in their hometown to close. According to the *Huntsville Daily Times*, the women had been unsuccessful in their job hunt. They returned to Huntsville aboard the freight train, where they encountered seven white boys. "Suddenly," the article reported, "the 12 negroes, brandishing their revolvers, leaped from a box car into the open car, cowered the white men in one corner and ordered them to leap from the train." All but two, O'Dell Gladwell and Orville Gilley, did as they were told. Gladwell, the newspaper report continued, was forced "onto the ladder of the car," struck in the head by "the butt end of a pistol," and fell to the ground, "landing so that he was not seriously injured. Gillie [Gilley] was allowed to remain on the car, after being invited by the black men to take part in the attack and refusing. He had to witness the crime." Of the twelve alleged rapists, nine were caught and, "after a night of terror during which a mob of infuriated citizens milled about . . . in a threatening mood," now sat in the Scottsboro jail, protected by "three companies of the Alabama National Guard." The nine youths would become known as the Scottsboro Boys. Three suspects, the article reported, managed to evade capture.

VOLUME 3—NUMBER 2.

NEGROES INDICTE[

GRAND JURY FINDS 20 INDICTMENTS AGAINST BLACKS CHARGED WITH RAPE OF TWO WHITE GIRLS ON TRAIN

NEG[RO] NOT GUILTY TO MOST SERIOUS [L]EGAL HISTORY OF THE COUNTY

[S]et For Next M[onth] at Scottsboro [in] Case; Troops [Guard] Alleged Rapists

[alo]ng with au [neg]ro men stoo[d] [l]ast Tuesday morn[ing] [m]ost serious charges know[n] [in] Alabama, rape. The negroes wer[e] [P]atterson, Eugene Williams, Charlie Weems [Roy Wilso]n, Andy Wrigh[t] [a]ll of whom ple[a] [name]d Victoria Pric[e]

[20] INDICTMENTS AGAINST NEGROES

[Ja]ckson County Grand jury went into session las[t] [Mon]day morning investigating the case and Tuesda[y] [m]orning reported twenty indictments for rape agains[t] the nine negroes. There were nine individual indictment[s] [a]gainst the negroes for the alleged rape of Victoria Pric[e] nine against them for the alleged rape of Ruby Bate[s] and two indictments against the whole nine negroes c[ol]-[lectively for the alleged rape of both Victoria Price an[d]

[Jack]son *County Sentinel*, dated April 2, 1931, reported that [nine blac]k youths were arrested in Paint Rock, Alabama, on [charges o]f raping two white women (on right). (The photo of the [newspap]er was taken February 10, 2010.)

ON CHARGES OF RAPE

LEGED NEGRO ATTACKERS AND THEIR VICTIMS

tured above are the nine
roes indicted on a charge
aping two white girls af-
they had thrown the
te boy companions of
girls off a Southern
ght train between Stev-
on and Scottsboro Wed-
day of last week. In the
to the negroes are seen
rded by soldiers with
omatic rifles and riot

The women's story was carried throughout Alabama and into neighboring states. Farther afield, the *New York Times* reported that both Gladwell and Gilley, as well as the other white youths, were being held in jail as witnesses and that all nine black men were charged with criminal assault, or rape—an offense that carried the death penalty if found guilty. In addition, Haywood Patterson and Eugene Williams, described in the women's hometown newspaper as "the worst negro characters in Chattanooga," would be charged with attempted murder after Ray Thurman, one of the white boys who jumped from the train, said "the [two] negroes fired at him five times" with pistols. The paper also revealed that Sheriff Wann claimed six of the men had "confessed to the crime."

The truth differed from the newspaper accounts. No one confessed—not exactly. Each youth, fearing his life was in jeopardy, maintained his innocence, but some cast blame on the others. The *Jackson County Sentinel* reported, "One of the younger negroes was taken out by himself and he confessed to the whole matter but said 'the others did it.'"

Alfred E. Hawkins, the Jackson County Circuit Court judge, said he would call a grand jury into session at once to review the evidence and promised that if it returned formal charges, "the negroes would be brought to trial immediately." Satisfied that justice would be served in a legal and swift manner, most of the citizens of Jackson County now saw no need to take the law into their own hands. Although a crowd still formed around the jail, it was orderly and no longer threatening. As the *Jackson County Sentinel* noted, "The general temper of the public seems to be that the negroes will be given a fair and lawful trial in the courts and that the ends of justice can be met best in this manner." Even so, Sheriff Wann, realizing his jail wasn't secure, had the National Guard take the nine accused to Gadsden, Alabama, some sixty miles away, for safekeeping while they awaited their trial in Scottsboro.

THE HIGHER COURT

Limbach

is 1931 image depicts a vulture ready to swoop down from e gallows to lynch, or hang, the nine youths accused of utally attacking and raping two white women. The accusation rape was often used as an excuse for white mobs to deliver nishment without the benefit of the courts. Although not stricted to the South, lynching was a way to intimidate blacks, pecially after the Civil War. Thousands of black people died at e hands of unruly, violent hordes for alleged crimes ranging m disrespecting a White person to horse thieving to murder.

A HOT TIME IN THE OLD TOWN

Judge Alfred E. Hawkins promised reporters and the citizens of Jackson County it would be a fair trial, one that would deliver speedy justice. But local citizens were more interested in speed—meaning the swiftness of punishment—than in fairness. There was no presumption of innocence until proved guilty in the minds of most locals or in the region's newspapers. The *Huntsville Daily Times* wrote, "On conviction of the nine brutes who have been protected by law since their apprehension, this newspaper joins with the public and the duly constituted authorities in seeing that the law is carried out to the letter." The editorial continued, "This was a heinous and unspeakable crime, unthinkable in its deplorable conduct and savored of the jungle, the way back dark ages of meanest African corruption. The white man will not stand for such acts."

Judge Hawkins was legally obligated to appoint lawyers to represent the Scottsboro Boys if he wanted the trial to appear to be anything more than a charade. There were seven lawyers in Scottsboro, and he assigned them all to the case. All but one, Milo C. Moody, found reasons they couldn't defend the boys.

Moody was just shy of his seventieth birthday when he agreed to take the case. One person noted that he was a "doddering, extremely unreliable, senile individual who is losing whatever ability he once had."

At Trial: Scottsboro

Alfred E. Hawkins, Jackson County Circuit Court judge

REPRESENTING THE STATE (THE PROSECUTION):
H. G. Bailey, Jackson County circuit solicitor

REPRESENTING THE NINE DEFENDANTS:
Stephen R. Roddy, * real estate attorney from Chattanooga, Tennessee; **Milo C. Moody**, local attorney assisting Roddy

WITNESSES FOR THE PROSECUTION:
Victoria Price, accuser; **Ruby Bates**, accuser; **Orville Gilley**, white hobo aboard the freight train; **M. L. Wann**, Jackson County sheriff; **Dr. R. R. Bridges** and **Dr. Marvin Lynch**, the two physicians who examined the women; **James Broadway**, passerby who joined the Paint Rock posse; **Ory Dobbins**, local resident

WITNESSES FOR THE DEFENSE:
only the defendants

* *Roddy's role was never confirmed by Judge Hawkins.*

Although he had a reputation for defending "unpopular ideas" in the past, Moody's main interest in the Scottsboro Boys wasn't justice or that he believed them to be innocent. Rather, the job carried with it a small fee.

In neighboring Tennessee, a Chattanooga physician became concerned that the youths wouldn't be treated fairly. Dr. P. A. Stephens called a meeting of the Interdenominational Colored Ministers' Alliance to discuss the young men's arrests. When members of the alliance learned that Mrs. Ada Wright, mother of Andy and Roy, attended one of their churches, they decided they should do something. By the evening of March 26, they had raised $50.08. The doctor approached Stephen R. Roddy, a local attorney who dealt mostly with real estate. Roddy was an unlikely choice because he had no experience in criminal law, but he was the only lawyer Stephens could think of who might consider the idea of working for such a small fee. Another shadow hanging over the selection was that Roddy had difficulty remaining sober. At first, Roddy was reluctant, but he eventually agreed to see what he could do for a total fee of $120.

Excitement filled the courtroom on Monday, March 30, the day of the grand jury hearing. Despite spectators crowding into the space, there was little to see. Under National Guard protection, the nine boys entered pleas of not guilty, and then the grand jury voted to go into closed-door hearings. Victoria Price and Orville Gilley were the only witnesses to testify. Within an hour, the grand jury had reached its decision to formally charge the nine. Judge Hawkins set the trial date for Monday, April 6, just twelve days after the alleged crime and one week after the grand jury hearing.

In Scottsboro, the first Monday of the month was known as Fair Day, a day when farmers from miles around brought their families to town to sell produce, exchange goods and gossip, and buy supplies. It was no different that first Monday in April but with the added attraction of a trial. By seven a.m., several thousand people—one report put the number at ten thousand—pushed into the square around the courthouse. Many spectators took positions on the rooftops of surrounding buildings to gain a better view of the spectacle. Clarence Norris later recalled, "the crowd was thick as hair on a dog's back." National Guardsmen kept the spectators away from the courthouse. As an extra precaution, more soldiers stood ready at four armed machine guns near the entrances to the building.

In a courtroom filled with white male onlookers, Judge Hawkins called the trial to order just before nine o'clock a.m. Immediately, there was confusion. Who was representing the nine accused: Milo Moody from Scottsboro or Stephen Roddy from Chattanooga?

Roddy, who had arrived earlier that morning amid a barrage of hostile insults from the crowd outside the courthouse, already had downed several alcoholic drinks—so many that he was described by a member of the prosecution team as being unable to walk straight. When Hawkins asked if he would be defending the nine, Roddy would not say what his role was. "I am here," he said, "but not as employed counsel by these defendants, but [by] people who are interested in them." When Roddy admitted to being both unprepared and unfamiliar with Alabama law, Moody stepped up and said he would be willing to assist him with the defense.

With no preparation and only a thirty-minute interview with the boys, in which he asked "which ones did the raping," Roddy opened for the defense. The first thing he attempted was to have the trial moved from Scottsboro, arguing that articles in the local newspapers had prejudiced potential jury members against the youths. One editorial maintained that the "claim is without foundation at all. . . . We tried very hard to temper the story down to keep from inciting the people." Yet, the editor continued, "The evidence against them is corroborated and witnessed."

Roddy failed to call any witnesses other than Sheriff Wann to support his request for a change of venue. But the sheriff, who only days earlier had felt the need to phone the governor and ask for the National Guard in order to prevent a mob lynching, now changed his story. Suddenly, he denied that any threats had been made or that he'd had to defend his prisoners from an angry mob. He agreed with the prosecution that the Scottsboro Boys would receive a fair trial in Jackson County. Judge Hawkins denied Roddy's request.

The preliminary details out of the way, circuit solicitor H. G. Bailey, who handled the prosecution for the state, decided to hold four trials. The first to be tried would be Clarence Norris and Charlie Weems, followed by Haywood Patterson, who would be tried alone. Next Olen Montgomery, Ozie Powell, Willie Roberson, Andy Wright, and Eugene Williams would all face a jury together. The last of the lot and the youngest, Roy Wright, would have his own trial.

By two thirty that afternoon, an all-white, all-male jury had been selected, and Bailey called his first witness to the stand in the trial against Norris and Weems. Victoria Price wore a new dress, furnished by the owners of one of Huntsville's mills, when she took the witness chair that afternoon. She testified that she and Ruby Bates had gone to Chattanooga to look for work in the cotton mills on Tuesday, March 24, and stayed with Mrs. Callie Brochie, who ran a boardinghouse five blocks from the railroad yards. The pair looked for work on Wednesday morning and, finding none, decided to return to Huntsville aboard the Chattanooga to Memphis freight train. At first, according to Price, everything had gone smoothly. She and Bates took shelter in a railcar already occupied at one end by seven white fellows. But as the train dipped down into Alabama from Tennessee, a dozen black men, each one brandishing an open knife and two with pistols, swarmed over the side of the car. She said the Negroes ordered all but one of the white hoboes to jump off the train and then overpowered

The Wisdom of Men?

Although women throughout the United States gained the right to vote in 1920, those in Alabama couldn't sit on juries until 1957, when three were chosen to serve on a jury in a US district court. The US district court was subject to the federal law signed that same year allowing women to serve as jurors in federal trials. Considered the property of their husbands, much like livestock or farming equipment, Alabama women weren't allowed to sit on state court juries until 1966. Men of the time generally regarded women as the weaker—both physically and mentally—of the sexes and thought women belonged in the home, raising children and looking after their husbands. They listed many reasons women should be excluded from jury duty, but one of the most common excuses was that women were too delicate to hear the sordid details of criminal trials.

her and Bates, tearing off their clothes and holding knives to their throats. Price knew how to tell a story, one that both engaged and enraged the white men who filled the court that day in Scottsboro. In the hushed courtroom, she pointed out the six who she claimed had raped her. About the testimony, Norris later wrote, the women "took the stand. . . . and lied and lied." He continued, "They said we used knives and hit them up the side of the head with guns to make them have sex. But the law never found no knives or guns on us because we didn't have any."

Roddy, upon cross-examination, tried to discredit the twice-married Price by attempting to show she was not the innocent young woman she portrayed. A divorced woman was thought by many to be a person without morals or one who wasn't worthy of respect. (A divorced man, meanwhile, wasn't held in such contempt.) But with each attempt to damage Price's character, Bailey objected, and Judge Hawkins upheld the objection. When Roddy tried to probe into the woman's past by asking whether she'd ever been arrested or in jail, the prosecution again raised an objection. Once more, Judge Hawkins sustained it. It was clear the judge was not going to allow that line of questioning. The reputation of a white woman was not going to be tarnished in his courtroom.

As his next witness, Bailey called one of the two doctors who had examined Price and Bates within an hour and a half of the alleged rapes. Dr. R. R. Bridges testified that both women showed evidence of having had sexual relations at some time before their examinations, but he couldn't be more specific than that. His testimony was enough, however, to make an impression on judge and jury. What went almost without notice, especially by Roddy and Moody, was the doctor's statement that neither woman looked as if she'd been brutally attacked and beaten. Price claimed she'd been hit on the side of the head with the butt end of a pistol, but the doctor found no such wound. Neither woman was hysterical, and beyond a few minor scratches and bruises, both appeared in good condition. On cross-examination, neither of the two defense lawyers questioned Bridges about any of his medical findings. When Roddy, who acted

Victoria Price stuck to her story and proved to be a tougher
witness under cross-examination than defense attorneys thought.

as the lead defense attorney, asked almost anything of the state's witnesses, Bailey objected. Judge Hawkins usually sided with the state and found the prosecutor's objections valid. Objection after objection, sustained.

When Dr. Marvin Lynch, the second doctor to examine Price and Bates, took the witness chair, he revealed the same findings as Bridges: no evidence of violence or brutality.

Judge Hawkins adjourned the court for the day.

When the trial resumed the next day, it was Ruby Bates's turn to tell her story. While Price had been unruffled and quick with answers to questions put to her, Bates was uncertain and often hesitant. She repeated what Price had said about the purpose of their trip to Chattanooga and staying at Mrs. Brochie's boardinghouse, but when it came to the white boys at the other end of the freight car, their stories differed. Price had said one of the white fellows had helped them board the train and that they'd talked with them for some time before the fight with the black youths broke out. Bates claimed that she and Price remained at the other end of the car and shared no conversation with the boys. Her version of the fight was also different. Price said the Negroes had boarded the freight car all at once with knives and guns flashing. Bates, on the other hand, testified that only two came into the car at first, and they began arguing with the white youths. When several other black men got into the car, they told the white men to get off. Four of them jumped off the freight train without a fuss. Only three white boys resisted the black youths' demands. When she described the alleged rape, she said simply that one threatened her with a knife and another with a gun. A third, she said, attacked her.

Roddy, for the defense, asked why she had said nothing at first about the rape when everyone was taken off the train in Paint Rock. He indicated that all she told the deputy sheriff was that a fight had broken out between "the colored boys and the white boys." He suggested that she and Price were traveling with some of the white boys and that she was concerned they might be charged with vagrancy or being without a home or a job. Where women were concerned, vagrancy also implied prostitution. Bates denied the charge, and Roddy failed to press the matter.

After Bates's testimony, Bailey called other witnesses. Some were more helpful to the prosecution than others. James Broadway, a passerby who had joined the posse, recalled that Price hadn't made any complaint about the nine black defendants until some time after she'd been taken from the train. Another witness testified that he had seen a scuffle aboard the train from the loft of his barn, some thirty yards from the tracks.

Bailey rested the prosecution's case.

Now it was Roddy's turn to try to defend Norris and Weems. Unfortunately, he had no witnesses to call other than the defendants themselves. He called Charles Weems to the witness chair.

A lanky youth well over six feet tall, Weems could barely read or write. He had stopped school in the fifth grade to begin a life of hoboing. Among a family of ten, only he and one brother were still alive, but he had not seen his brother in years.

Weems readily admitted there had been a scuffle with some white boys who had tried to knock Haywood Patterson off the oil tanker Patterson had been riding on, but added that it hadn't been much of a fight. After Patterson hit one of the boys, the white fellows began jumping off the train, according to Weems. By the time Orville Gilley decided he would leap from the train, it was going downhill and had gained speed. Weems and Patterson worried that Gilley would be hurt, so they pulled him back in the car.

Solicitor Bailey fired question after question at Weems, but the young man stood firm, telling the lawyer he didn't know there had been any women on the train. He said the only other people in the car with him were Patterson, some other Negroes who jumped off before they reached Paint Rock, and the white boy they'd kept from leaving the train. He offered nothing to support his testimony other than his word that he was telling the truth.

Clarence Norris then took the stand. Norris had attended school sporadically for three or four years and had never learned to read or write. By age thirteen he was helping his father with full-time farm work, but Norris didn't like farming. He left home at fifteen to ride the rails, returning home briefly in 1929. His father died shortly after his return, and when his mother moved in with some relatives after that, he resumed wandering across the Southeast by rail.

Norris was nervous as he testified. He verified Weems's account of the fight, but it didn't take long for Bailey to shake the defendant. By the third question, Norris was so rattled that he confessed to watching from the top of the neighboring car as the other eight Negroes attacked the girls. Roddy objected, trying to quiet the youth on the witness stand, but Norris plunged ahead with his accusations against the others. The defense now in tatters, Roddy requested a brief recess, during which he pleaded with Bailey to accept guilty pleas in exchange for life sentences. But Bailey, even more confident of convictions and the death penalty, rejected the offer.

Within an hour of instructing the jury in the Weems and Norris proceedings, Judge Hawkins began the trial against Haywood Patterson. One trial after the other. Like most of the other eight boys, Patterson had little formal education. The son of a Georgia sharecropper, he'd left school after the third grade. He worked in the steel mills and as a delivery boy in Chattanooga for a time, but had been riding the rails since he was fourteen. By 1931, he'd had a few minor encounters with the Chattanooga police, and most whites took an immediate dislike to him because of his disrespectful attitude, which didn't fit with the way white Southerners thought they should be treated.

As Price testified in the Patterson trial, she told the same story she'd related earlier but now added embellishments. Seeming to enjoy the attention the case was bringing her, she recalled that Patterson had had one of the guns and Weems the other. She also testified that they fired one or two shots but was no longer certain that each of the black youths had wielded a knife. She specifically identified Patterson, though, as one of the Negroes who had raped her.

When it was Roddy's turn to question Price, he tried once again to attack her reputation by suggesting she worked from time to time as a prostitute. Although the prosecution objected and the judge sustained his objection, Price became angered and answered anyway: "I have not had intercourse with any other white man but my husband; I want you to distinctly understand that." Roddy had no further questions for Victoria Price.

Bailey hoped that Ruby Bates would confirm Price's claim of rape by Patterson, so he called her to the stand next. After first telling the prosecutor that she thought Patterson might have been the first to assault the older girl, she was less certain of the details when questioned by Roddy.

As Bates was excused from the witness chair, the bailiff approached Judge Hawkins. He told the judge that the jury in the Weems and Norris trial had reached its verdict. Judge Hawkins had Patterson's jury taken out of the courtroom to an adjacent area, and the other jury entered. The room, deadly silent now, awaited the verdict.

"We find the defendants," the court clerk read from the paper the jury foreman had handed him, "guilty of rape and fix their sentence at death."

The spectators in the courtroom erupted in a roar of applause and cheers. Outside, in the town square, a crowd of some fifteen hundred people waited for news of a verdict on this second day of the Scottsboro Boys' trials. When they heard the commotion coming from inside the courthouse, they knew that Weems and Norris had been found guilty. They, too, burst into an enthusiastic clamor. Adding to the day's excitement, the Ford Motor Company was parading its new line of trucks around the square. To attract people to inspect the caravan of automobiles, an amplifier blared out a popular tune, "There'll Be a Hot Time in the Old Town Tonight." The exuberance from inside and outside the courthouse spilled into the room where the Patterson jury waited, and Roddy tried to capitalize on it. He asked Judge Hawkins to declare a mistrial, to invalidate the proceedings against Patterson, because his jury now knew that the first of the boys to be tried had been found guilty. The judge denied his request.

When Patterson's trial resumed, Bailey called the two doctors, both of whom repeated their earlier testimony. A new witness, Ory Dobbins (sometimes referred to as Robbins), testified that while "standing at the woodpile [at his house], about a hundred yards from the track," he'd seen a colored man grab a woman and throw her down into the bed of a railcar. Roddy had no questions.

As in the first trial, Roddy had no witnesses to call other than the defendant himself. But Patterson's testimony was confusing and contradictory. He at first denied taking part in the fight, saying, "I was not with the other boys who took part in the fight." He said that he'd witnessed the scuffle between some white boys and twelve Negroes from an adjacent railcar. When Bailey questioned him, Patterson said he'd seen Price assaulted by the other black youths, but that he, Eugene Williams, and Andy and Roy Wright had not been part of it. Minutes later, however, he denied he'd confessed to seeing any girls on the train. Years later Patterson recalled, "I saw nobody ravish nobody. I was in a fight. That's all. Just a fight with white boys. . . . I saw no girl. I raped nobody."

To buttress Patterson's contradictory story, Roddy called thirteen-year-old Roy Wright. He described a brief struggle with several white boys and said the black boys had taken pity on Orville Gilley and pulled him back into the railcar so he wouldn't get hurt. Then he demolished any hope Roddy may have had about his testimony bolstering Patterson's. He told the jury that he saw "nine negroes down there [in the railcar] with the girls and all had intercourse with them. . . . I saw that with my own eyes." Continuing his testimony, he added, "Five of these men here"—meaning the defendants excluding himself, his brother, Williams, and Patterson—assaulted the girls. Roy's statements not only cast doubt on Patterson's claim that he had not seen any girls until Paint Rock but also made it appear as if all the young men were lying.

What Roy did not tell the court that day was that a deputy sheriff had asked whether he was going to be a witness for the prosecution. When he said no, he was taken out of the court during a recess to a room, where the guards, he said, "whipped me and it seemed like they was going to kill me. All the time they kept saying, 'Now will you tell?' and finally it seemed like I couldn't stand no more and I said yes. Then I went back into the courtroom . . . and I said I had seen Charlie Weems and Clarence Norris . . . with the white girls."

Wednesday, April 8, the third day of trials, began with a continuation of the Patterson hearing. The case was given to the jury at around eleven a.m., and the jury reached its decision in less than twenty-five minutes: guilty. The jury sentenced him to death. Unlike at the first trial, the spectators in the courtroom remained silent as the verdict was read. Judge Hawkins had ordered twenty-five armed guardsmen to stand throughout the room to make sure there were no demonstrations. Years after the hearing and judgment, Patterson wrote, "I was convicted in their minds before I went on trial. . . . All that spoke for me on that witness stand was my black skin—which didn't do so good."

The trial of Ozie Powell, Willie Roberson, Andy Wright, Eugene Williams, and Olen Montgomery began fifteen minutes after the Patterson trial ended. Victoria Price took the witness stand for the third time in as many days. Once again, she added even more graphic details to the versions of the story she'd told during her first two appearances in court. "The first one of these five defendants that put his hands on me," she testified, "was the one sitting there with the sleepy eyes, Olen Montgomery; he ravished me." She alleged that "Eugene Williams said if we told it any way at all he would kill us."

Although Price had told the court during the Patterson trial that the boys had fired one or possibly two shots over her head to make her give in to their demands, during Roddy's cross-examination she now claimed, "I didn't testify yesterday there was only one shot. I know what I said yesterday. I say today there—seven shots fired in all, from the time the racket started until it ended." She also recalled that "it took three of them to get off my overalls. . . . I saw knives in the hands of every one except two, and they had guns." Weems, she said, was the ringleader, but the others all participated.

Ruby Bates's testimony also did not agree with what she'd said on the witness stand previously. During the Patterson trial, she had said two black youths entered the railcar at first before the others joined. Now she said, "They all came over in a bunch." Bates's version of events now was closer to Price's—but only after the two had spent another night together in custody. Like Price, Bates had been wearing overalls and a shirt on March 25, the day the girls said they were raped. Over this she wore a coat and had on a hat, but she maintained, "My overalls were taken off me. None of my other clothes were taken off; just the overalls. The colored boys ravished me then." But as on March 26, when the nine stood before her in the Scottsboro jail lineup, she still could not identify which, if any, of the youths were her attackers. She refused to point the finger of blame.

Ozie Powell was the first of the five boys to take the witness chair for the defense that day. His story had been mostly consistent throughout the ordeal: "I did not see no women until I got to Paint Rock. . . . I did not have a knife. The officers searched me and didn't find a knife. I did not have a pistol. I had not thrown away a knife. I did not even have any knife." Prosecutor Bailey could not shake Powell's testimony. Nor was he successful at getting any of the other youths on trial that day to change their stories.

"I am the boy," said Willie Roberson, taking the stand later, "that the doctor testified was suffering from syphilis and gonorrhea. . . . I have chancres. They are swollen and sore. I could not have intercourse. I am in such shape that I could not have intercourse."

Andy Wright took the witness chair next, saying, "I did not even see a woman on the train; I saw them after I got to Paint Rock; I saw two there, the two women who are here in the court. That is the first time I had seen them."

Olen Montgomery also declared his innocence: "I did not have anything to do with raping those girls; I had not seen them. If I had seen them, [I] would not have known whether they were men or women; I cannot see good."

Finally, Eugene Williams spoke: "I did not see any girls until we got to Paint Rock. A fight took place there in the gondola [open railcar]; we fought those white boys. I do not know how many white boys there were, about seven or eight. There were eight or nine of us boys. The girls were not in there. I did not see the girls at all until we got to Paint Rock."

To wrap up the case against the five boys, the prosecution called Orville Gilley to the witness chair for the first time since the grand jury.

Gilley testified that he was on the train the day of the alleged rape. Although Roddy objected, the prosecution asked Gilley whether he had seen any of the five young men on trial in the railcar. Judge Hawkins overruled Roddy's objection, and the witness answered, "I saw every one of those five in the gondola." When asked if he saw the girls in the same car, Gilley answered, "Yes, sir."

Roddy didn't cross-examine the witness, nor did he offer a closing argument in this or in any of the hearings held so far. The case was given to the jury at 4:20 p.m. Solicitor Bailey was eager to conclude the trials against the nine youths, but Roy Wright was only thirteen. Alabama law required him to be tried as a juvenile unless the state, represented by Bailey, brought special proceedings to waive that condition. To expedite things, Bailey was willing to compromise— life imprisonment instead of the death sentence—in exchange for a guilty plea. Roddy declined the offer. He at least knew enough about criminal law to be aware that a guilty plea would surrender Wright's chances to appeal. The Roy Wright trial was brief and without much in the way of a defense. Again, Roddy made no closing statement, made no effort to convince the jury of the thirteen-year-old's innocence. Bailey, as he had in the other trials, asked the jury to find Wright guilty. But instead of asking for the death penalty, he asked for only a life sentence, given Wright's age.

By nine o'clock that evening the juries in the two cases had not reached a decision. Both juries retired for the night, but on Thursday morning the jury for the five reported its verdict: guilty. As in the two previous cases, this jury settled on the death penalty for each of the defendants. At two o'clock that afternoon, the jury weighing the Roy Wright case reported that it could not reach a verdict. Despite Bailey's request for a life sentence, "the jury stood eleven to one in favor of the death penalty." Judge Hawkins declared a mistrial, but this did not mean that Roy was free.

Four days. Four trials. Nine youths. Eight guilty verdicts. One mistrial.

Clarence Norris recalled, "Judge Hawkins sentenced us to die April 9, 1931. The eight of us stood before him. He asked us if we had anything to say." Despite a report in the *Progressive Age* that all the defendants answered no to the question, Haywood Patterson remembered that he spoke up, saying, "Yes, I have something to say. I'm not guilty of this charge." Regardless, Judge Hawkins voiced the same words eight times to the eight boys before him: "In Keeping with the Verdict of the jury, I pronounce the sentence of death by electrocution on July 10th, 1931 and may the Lord have Mercy on your soul."

After the sentencing, military guards returned the boys to the Gadsden jail. Patterson remembered they could "see where an old gallows was rigged up. Must have gone back to the slavey [*sic*] days." Unhappy with the prison food and the way the trials had gone, the eight soon kicked up a fuss. "Bring me some pork chops," demanded Patterson. "We're going to die and we can have anything we want." Thinking the boys might be plotting an escape, the sheriff called in extra guards, but as Patterson told it, they got their pork chops. At some point, though, the guards grew "serious." He remembered: "The cell door banged open. They beat on us with their fists. They pushed us against the walls. They kicked and tramped about on our legs and feet." The *Huntsville Daily Times* summed up this event in a headline that read "Negroes Riot in Gadsden to Protest Doom." Young Roy Wright, sitting in a separate cell, wasn't part of the disturbance. The next day, handcuffed two by two and trussed together with rope, the nine boys were loaded into a truck and taken to the jail in Birmingham.

The 9 Scottsboro Boys Must Not Die!

STOP THE LEGAL LYNCHING!

Fellow Citizens:-

The lynch courts of Alabama handed down a lynch verdict for Haywood Patterson, first of the 9 innocent Negro boys framed up to burn in the electric chair.

THEY ARE TRYING TO LYNCH THE OTHER BOYS!

The fight of the Scottsboro Boys is our fight! They must be saved! Only mass protest of Negro and white workers will save the boys! WE MUST HAVE IMMEDIATE ACTION!

Wednesday, April 26th, 1933, 2000 marchers will come to Philadelphia from New York and New Jersey. They are marching to Washington to demand that President Roosevelt FREE the boys!

WELCOME THE MARCHERS JOIN IN THE PROTEST!

COME TO THE PROTEST OUTDOOR MEETING

WEDNESDAY, APRIL 26th, 6 P. M.

at 18th & Reed Sts.

PROMINENT SPEAKERS — (American Woodman's Band will play)

March to INDOOR PROTEST MEETING WEDNESDAY, APRIL 26th, 1933, 8 P. M. at JOHN SIMMONS MEMORIAL CHURCH, 18th & WHARTON STS.

Prominent Speakers — Prominent Pastors

Attorney David Levinson, Jennie Cooper, Dist. Sec'y. I.L.D. Scottsboro Marchers and others.

PROTEST!   ORGANIZE!   FIGHT!

THEY SHALL NOT DIE!

Multigraphed   Auspices: Scottsboro Defense Committee

What impressed the Scottsboro Boys and their parents about the International Labor Defense (ILD) and the Communist Party was that they organized rallies and marches in cities across the United States, while the NAACP, fearful of tarnishing its reputation, was slow to get involved.

4

A LEGAL LYNCHING

The case against the Scottsboro Boys was far from over. The day before the eight youths were sentenced on that Thursday, April 9, Judge Hawkins had received a telegram from the International Labor Defense (ILD), the legal branch of the Communist Party USA. The ILD was formed to oppose the Ku Klux Klan and to defend poor and working people. Whereas Alabama saw a fair and just trial, much of the rest of the country, including the ILD, didn't see it that way. The telegram accused the judge and the state of attempting to "legally lynch nine negro workers . . . on frame-up rape charges." The organization demanded an "immediate change of venue, new trial, [and] dismissal [of the] defense lawyers." A copy of the telegram was sent to Governor Benjamin Miller, and other telegrams, letters, and postcards soon followed, demanding a "new trial for the nine Negro youths railroaded to the electric chair in mock trial at Scottsboro" and "the immediate safe release of the nine innocent Scottsboro Negro Boys." It was a reaction the people of Alabama had not anticipated.

Black and white citizens in communities near and far had followed the Scottsboro case in newspapers. Some wondered why the National Association for the Advancement of Colored People (NAACP) wasn't involved in the boys' defense. The NAACP had

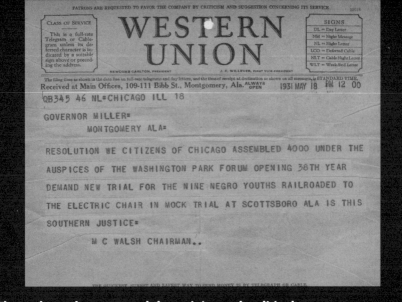

Throughout the country, labor, civic, and political groups, encouraged by the Communist Party USA, organized to accuse the state of Alabama of holding mock trials that railroaded the black youths known as the Scottsboro Boys to the electric chair.

The Communists used the Scottsboro trials and the fates of the nine black youths to shed light on how Negroes generally were treated in the United States. It encouraged members and others, both in the US and abroad, to demand freedom for the young men.

earned respect for defending black causes in the country's courts of law, but it was cautious and protective of its reputation. It was aware that Chattanooga's Interdenominational Colored Ministers' Alliance had hired Stephen Roddy, but "the last thing they wanted was to identify the Association with a gang of mass rapists unless they were reasonably certain the boys were innocent or that their constitutional rights had been abridged." The NAACP delayed taking action.

The day after Judge Hawkins sentenced the boys, however, Walter White, executive secretary of the association, began receiving telephone calls from NAACP branches around the country, as well as other organizations, liberal magazines, and progressive individuals, demanding that something be done to save the young men. Famed defense attorney Clarence Darrow was among those who telephoned. Darrow was a member of the NAACP's board of directors and an active member of the American Civil Liberties Union (ACLU), a group dedicated to defending the rights guaranteed every person by the US Constitution. He told White that Joseph Brodsky, the chief lawyer of the International Labor Defense, had asked him to join in the appeal of the boys' case to the Alabama Supreme Court. The Communist Party had long promoted racial equality as a way to attract black members. White cautioned Darrow to avoid the communist organization, saying its main goal was propaganda. Ever since the Russian Revolution of 1917, when workers violently took up arms against the wealthy ruling class and overpowered them, many of America's leaders—upon whom the NAACP depended for donations—looked upon the Communist Party with suspicion and distrust. White assured Darrow that the NAACP was already taking steps toward getting a new trial.

What White didn't understand was that since the guilty verdicts and death sentences had come down, the ILD had moved quickly. It viewed the Scottsboro case as a good public-relations tool, a way to recruit new members to the Communist Party. After Darrow declined to help, the ILD hired George W. Chamlee Sr. to represent the youths. Chamlee was a well-respected lawyer from a prominent Tennessee family. He was a competent lawyer, unlike Roddy and Moody, and with him on board, Brodsky went to Birmingham to interview the youths. As Patterson recalled, "Two guys from New York, head men from the International Labor Defense, brought us pops and candy and gave them to us boys in the visiting room." While White was trying, without a lot of success, to get copies of the Scottsboro trial transcripts, Brodsky was with the boys in person, promising them a vigorous defense by the best lawyers in the country. He obtained the signatures or marks (some of them could not write their own names) of all nine on documents that gave the ILD full control over their defense. Writing to the Alabama governor, the ILD demanded a stay—a postponement—of the scheduled July 10 execution set by Judge Hawkins so it could investigate the Scottsboro case and prepare an appeal.

To complicate White's belief that the NAACP would soon have the Scottsboro case under control, Brodsky reached out to as many parents as he could find and told them of the ILD's plans to defend their boys. He promised them the support of communists across the country and around the globe. It was an appreciated change. The parents had never been contacted by Roddy or by Chattanooga's Interdenominational Colored Ministers' Alliance. Claude and Janie Patterson, Ada Wright, and Mamie Williams all agreed that the ILD should represent their sons, who were minors. Brodsky arranged for Mr. Patterson, Mrs. Wright, and Mrs. Williams to visit their children for the first time since their arrests. Mr. Patterson told Haywood, "You will burn sure if you don't . . . trust in the International Labor Defense to handle the case." Ozie Powell's relatives seemed to agree, writing that they had "full confidence and agreement with the

50

The ILD and Communist Party sold sheets of stamps in varying denominations to help offset the expense of defending the Scottsboro Boys.

organization's handling of the case. . . . We realize that only mass protest of the working class . . . can save the boys from the electric chair." Yet Powell wrote to the NAACP's White on May 11 to say his mother had "advised me that I did right in signing the paper for you requesting the International Labor Defense to keep hands off. . . . I don't approve of the manner in which the International Labor Defense has handled things. . . . They have only been agitating. It has given them lots of publicity, which no doubt helped their personal gain. But does that really help us? I can't see where it does." He accused the ILD of "trying to poison our minds such as 'you being our *deadly enemy*,'" and added, "Clarence Norris feels the same as I." In its effort to convince the youths to settle on the ILD rather than the NAACP for legal representation, the communist organization began sending each family a small allowance.

On April 27, all the boys except Roy Wright were taken to Alabama's death house, Kilby Prison, near Montgomery, the state capital. As Clarence Norris later described it, "There were sixteen cells, eight on each side of a narrow hallway. At the end of the hall was a green door and behind it was the electric chair. There was a full house, with two and three men to a cell, all black. . . . I was put into a cage with Olen Montgomery. This was good because he could read and write for me and he didn't mind doing it." Haywood Patterson, in a separate cell, sometimes got so worried and scared that he would sweat until his clothes were soaked. He recalled, "When they turned on the juice [to the chair] . . . we could hear the z-z-z-z-z-z of the electric current."

In the request for a new trial, the ILD, represented by Chamlee and Brodsky, and the NAACP appeared at a hearing before Judge Hawkins on June 5, 1931. The NAACP's White had hired the Birmingham law firm of Fort, Beddow, and Ray to represent the boys for the NAACP, but Roderick Beddow and Ben Ray wanted to keep their firm's connection to the case as low profile as possible. The plan was for Roddy and Moody to remain, but for Beddow to supervise them. Moody, however, withdrew from the case, leaving Roddy, who now made demands for excessive amounts of money. His main interest was to defend not the boys but himself. The ILD had attacked his legal skills and professionalism.

The attorneys from both camps argued that the boisterous mob that surrounded the courthouse the day the verdicts came down in the Weems and Norris trial had influenced the other juries. The jury members, who now had taken the witness stand, denied that the clamor had affected their decisions. But when Chamlee attempted to ask whether racial prejudice had shaped their verdicts, Judge Hawkins wouldn't allow it. Roddy was so rattled he didn't bother to ask any questions at all of the former jurors.

Chamlee and Brodsky submitted into evidence a collection of signed statements disputing the reputations of Price and Bates as the fine examples of southern womanhood the prosecution had painted during the trial. Both, according to the affidavits, were known prostitutes who socialized with blacks, a taboo in southern polite society. Although the state's attorney disputed this portrayal of its star witnesses, the findings were backed up by other investigations, including that of J. A. Hackworth of the Hackworth Detective Agency in Huntsville. It was a bold move for Chamlee and Brodsky to cast doubt on the truthfulness of two white women of the South, and news of this development quickly spread beyond the courthouse. Stepping outside after the hearing, Chamlee and Brodsky were met by a crowd of men who told them to get out of town if they knew what was good for them. They got out of town.

The defendants and their parents had changed their minds so often about whom would represent them that it became difficult for the ILD and NAACP to know exactly what anybody wanted. By late May, the defendants had divided into two camps: Patterson, the Wright brothers, Eugene Williams, and Olen Montgomery favored the ILD; Ozie Powell, Charlie Weems, and Clarence Norris leaned to the NAACP. Willie Roberson seemed to change his mind and allegiance by the day, if not the hour. In frustration, the NAACP asked Clarence Darrow to join the case. Darrow was seventy-four and in failing health, but he found the $5,000 fee the NAACP offered attractive. Like the vast majority of Americans during the Great Depression, he was in need of money, despite his renown. Although Darrow deeply believed the ILD would jeopardize the case, he agreed to make one of the arguments before the Alabama Supreme Court. In September, the NAACP announced that he had been retained. The ILD saw Darrow's entry into the case for what it was—an attempt by the NAACP to gain control, to strengthen its position with the defendants.

In June, Janie Patterson and three other mothers of the young men had written that "every single one of those boys in Kilby Prison is with the ILD." Whether this was the case or not, Darrow's entry into the NAACP defense team caused Roberson finally to settle on the association. He wrote to White to say, "i want you have my case. . . . So if you are going to take my Case ples Right and let Me know." He had little education and his letter contained numerous errors. He signed his name "Willie Robinson" instead of Roberson, his actual name. Clarence Norris affirmed his stand with the NAACP. In August, he wrote, "It has been sometime since I have gotten a letter from you[.] But I want you to know that I am depending on you to fight my case. The I.L.D. is trying to get us but I think that you can do us more good than they can." That same month Claude Patterson, who had never wavered from wanting the ILD to defend his son, Haywood, checked in with White to register his opinion against the

NAACP: "I learned you was down there [at Kilby Prison] teachering the boys. . . . We don't need you and none your crowd for nothing for all you all is no good."

Darrow was still not keen to be connected with the communists. A *New York Times* article dated December 30, 1931, reported that a disagreement had arisen between Darrow and the ILD. Darrow was willing to separate himself from the NAACP and simply take the case as a private lawyer. He proposed that Chamlee and Brodsky do the same with regard to the ILD and the Communist Party. The two ILD lawyers rejected Darrow's proposal. The ILD wanted everyone to know that it was supporting the defense of the Scottsboro Boys. Darrow and his team would have no part in it. As the article reported, "Mr. Darrow declared he would not consider entering the case in any connection with any Communist organization." After his departure, all eight youths in Kilby Prison issued a statement through the *Daily Worker*, the newspaper of the Communist Party USA, which said that they had "made a written contract retaining George W. Chamlee, of Chattanooga, and Joseph D. Brodsky [*sic*] and their associates, as our attorneys to make motions for a new trial." White wrote to Roberson and Weems in early January 1932 to say, "You have chosen your counsel and that settles the matter so far as the N.A.A.C.P. is concerned. . . . You and the other boys have vacillated, changing your minds so frequently that it [is] impossible for any organization or individual to know what you do want." The NAACP was off the case.

REPRIEVE

Judge Hawkins, most newspaper editorials, and citizens throughout the state thought the Scottsboro trials had been fair and something of which Alabama could be justly proud. Even so, the judge set aside the execution date, pending an appeal to the Alabama Supreme Court. For unknown reasons, the Scottsboro Boys didn't learn about this development until seventy-two hours—just three days—before their scheduled date with Kilby Prison's electric chair on July 10. Haywood Patterson recalled: "July came very quick. About three days before I was due to die I got a letter from my people. They wrote that the I.L.D. lawyers got a stay of execution because they were carrying the case up the courts. I passed on the word to the fellows and they broke out in high talk. You would think the prison officials would have hipped [informed] us to this news, but they never said a word. It looked like they wanted to fret us to death if they couldn't get us any other way."

George Chamlee had no real hope that the Alabama Supreme Court would overturn the convictions handed down in Scottsboro. But it was a necessary step to get the case to the US Supreme Court. This is what Patterson meant when he said the ILD would carry "the case up the courts."

The *Press-Forum Weekly* of Mobile, Alabama, reported, "The forces fighting for the release of the nine Scottsboro boys and the forces attempting to burn these boys in the electric chair as a 'warning to Negro workers,' came to grips last week with the hearing before the Supreme Court of Alabama for a new trial for the defendants." The appeal began on January 21, 1932, when Alabama chief justice John C. Anderson responded to attempts of the ILD to influence the court. In the days and weeks leading up to the proceedings, the ILD had urged communists from around the globe and anyone else who thought the eight young men had been "railroaded to the electric chair in [a] mock trial" to inundate the court and the governor's office with messages. "Letters and telegrams of a highly revolutionary nature designed to intimidate the court's decision had flooded his office," Anderson told the crowded courtroom, but he promised the "court would do its duty regardless of outside pressure and confine itself strictly to the law in its deliberations on this case."

Charging that local newspapers had whipped up a lynching atmosphere against the nine youths, Chamlee opened the appeal by reading an article from the *Jackson County Sentinel* that supported his argument. He went on to say that the defense counsel had been unprepared and inadequate in the Scottsboro trials. Indeed, one of his main points was that Stephen Roddy had maintained from the beginning of those trials that he had not been hired to represent the Negroes. Chamlee accused Judge Hawkins of treating the subject of the boys' representation too lightly. They had been brought to trial without ever meeting with an attorney. "Throughout the trial," Chamlee told the justices, "there was a total disregard of the legal rights of the defendants. . . . The trial court abused its discretion in forcing the defendants to trial without preparation, witnesses or other assistance."

THEY MUST NOT DIE!

Against Race Discrimination!

Against Lynching!

... Postal Card ...

PLACE STAMP HERE

I demand the immediate safe release of the nine innocent Scottsboro Negro Boys.

Name *Bertha Markowitz*

Address *1084 New York Av*

Brooklyn N.Y.

38

To

Governor B. M. Miller

MONTGOMERY,

ALA.

PRINTED BY INTERNATIONAL LABOR DEFENSE

After the Scottsboro verdicts, postcards like this one sent from Bertha Markowitz flooded into the offices of both Governor Benjamin Meeks Miller and Judge Alfred E. Hawkins.

As he had done at the hearing before Judge Hawkins in June 1931, Chamlee presented the court with signed affidavits that cast a shadow on the reputations of Victoria Price and Ruby Bates. Additionally, there was new evidence: Percy Ricks, the fireman of the freight train, declared in a statement that the girls were in a boxcar and not in the car in which the boys had been riding.

Joseph Brodsky, however, presented most of the defense argument, and it revolved around the fairness of the Scottsboro trials. Not surprisingly, he agreed with Chamlee that the youths' legal rights had been ignored and abused. He insisted that the "mob spirit and hysteria" around the Scottsboro courthouse after the first verdict had "terrorized the judge, jury and defending counsel" to the point that fairness and impartiality in the other trials could not be achieved. Then he took up the issue of Alabama's all-white juries. He held that because no blacks had served on the juries, it prevented the defendants from receiving trials before their peers or even before anything that resembled the general makeup of the state. According to the ILD lawyer, this was a violation of the Fourteenth Amendment to the Constitution of the United States, which guarantees equal protection under the law and requires states, under its due process clause, to ensure that defendants have adequate representation by a lawyer. He stressed that the hurried speed with which the trials had been conducted also proved the trials were unfair. A speedy trial, as guaranteed by the Constitution, was one thing, but these trials, Brodsky contended, had been hurried to the point that Roy Wright, who should have been tried in a juvenile court because of his age, was tried in the same court as the other defendants and almost sentenced to death. But perhaps his most striking argument was that Eugene Williams, close in age to Roy, "was convicted in a court without jurisdiction over [juveniles]."

Attorney General Thomas Knight Jr. had higher political ambitions and used the trials of the Scottsboro Boys toward that end. In 1935, he became the state's thirteenth lieutenant governor.

Attorney General Thomas E. Knight Jr. argued about each of the defense lawyers' points. Knight, whose father was one of the associate justices sitting on the Alabama Supreme Court, contended, "there is no race prejudice in Alabama." He then "proceeded to call the boys 'niggers' and to state that there was no mob spirit in the Scottsboro case, the jury being totally uninfluenced by the newspapers."

In the end, the Alabama high court, by a six-to-one vote of the justices, upheld the convictions and sentences of seven of the eight defendants on March 24, 1932. Justice Thomas E. Knight Sr. wrote the majority opinion, which held "that the speed of the trial was no ground for reversal." Indeed, he suggested, it was just the opposite: "If there were more speed and less delay in the administration of the criminal laws of the land, life and property would be infinitely safer and greater respect would the criminally inclined have for the law." The court entirely brushed aside Brodsky's Fourteenth Amendment argument that the all-white juries deprived the defendants of equal protection and due process, saying, "The State of Alabama has the right . . . to fix the qualifications for jurors." Only the conviction of Eugene Williams "was reversed on the grounds he was a minor delinquent at the time of the alleged assault." Like Roy Wright, who remained in the Birmingham jail awaiting a new trial in juvenile court, Williams shouldn't have been tried as an adult. Once again, Ozie Powell, Willie Roberson, Andy Wright, Olen Montgomery, Charles Weems, Clarence Norris, and Haywood Patterson were sentenced to death. The Alabama Supreme Court set a new date for executing the young men in the state's electric chair, May 13, 1932.

The lone dissenting opinion was that of Chief Justice Anderson, who said, "In justice to the defendants and to the fair name of Alabama as well as the County of Jackson, these cases should be retried." Privately, Anderson confided to Walter White that he thought the flood of communist propaganda had hurt the defense's case.

Under Alabama law, Chamlee and Brodsky had just fifteen days to petition the Alabama Supreme Court to rehear their arguments. Chamlee announced that the paperwork was already in the works, as they planned to take the case all the way to the Supreme Court of the United States.

The Alabama Supreme Court had spoken. The Scottsboro trials were fair, even if the rest of the country didn't agree. It was no surprise that the court was bombarded with protests after its decision. In an unprecedented and likely illegal move, Knight, the attorney general, "issued a formal warning to telegraph companies in the State that they would be cited for contempt of court if any more coercive telegrams are delivered to the Alabama Supreme Court." Although he couldn't threaten US mail carriers who delivered letters and postcards of protest about the alleged legal lynching of the seven youths, he could at least try to intimidate telegraph companies. He maintained the telegrams were "illegal, libelous, scandalous, and . . . under the peculiar circumstances, obscene."

In a political move meant to embarrass the United States, the Communist Party USA encouraged communists throughout Europe to show their support for the Scottsboro Boys and to protest the "gross race prejudice and injustice against the Negro" that existed in the country, especially in the South. Demonstrations erupted in Germany and France. Editorials in British newspapers and others exposed the unfairness of the American court system, in so far as black citizens were concerned, and condemned the trials. When news of these events landed in Scottsboro, it both unsettled and agitated local residents. Responding to an editorial in the *Manchester Guardian*, a British newspaper, Scottsboro attorney James M. Proctor defended the legal process:

I have just read your editorial article concerning the so-called "Scottsboro Case." This article is so devoid of truth and fact that I wish to call your attention to the marked injustice you have done us in this instance. . . .

The truth about these cases is that the negro defendants were not "innocent children convicted on fake testimony by a race-prejudiced Court and jury," but, upon the other hand, are past the age of childish pranks and were convicted by the most damaging testimony I have ever heard in a court of justice. . . . Had we desired to prevent a fair and impartial trial, free from the world-wide abuse that has been heaped upon us, we could easily have lynched them without going into court.

The Alabama Supreme Court postponed the boys' date of execution so their attorneys could petition the Supreme Court of the United States. Before the US Supreme Court will hear an appeal, attorneys must convince the nine justices that the case involves an issue of constitutional law. The ILD hired Walter Pollak, a Harvard Law School graduate and eminent civil rights attorney, to make their case. In a preliminary hearing on May 27, 1932, he presented a set of facts he thought supported the ILD's position for seeking a new trial and tied these facts to the Constitution. The Supreme Court agreed to hear the case.

In the October 1932 session of the US Supreme Court, in a case that became known as *Powell v. Alabama*, named after Ozie Powell, Pollak argued the same points that had been presented at the Alabama Supreme Court, stressing that there had not been any Negroes on any of the juries and that the boys had been denied their right to choose their own legal representation. In Washington, DC, to support the state's Supreme Court justices who had reviewed the case and ruled that the Scottsboro trials were fair, Attorney General Knight justified the exclusion of blacks from the juries by pointing out that the defense attorneys hadn't objected at the time the jurors were chosen. He insisted that all due processes of law had been followed and that neither he nor the state had apologies to make. "The mere fact that negroes are not on a jury," he argued, "does not entitle the defendant to have . . . a motion for a new trial granted. There must be proof . . . that the jury commissioners purposely omitted" Negroes from the jury lists "because of their race or color." As to Pollak's point that the young men had not been allowed lawyers of their own choosing in the Scottsboro trials, Knight responded by writing that the youths "were not denied the right of counsel." They were represented, according to the attorney general, "by counsel from Chattanooga." Not mentioning Roddy's fondness for alcohol or Moody's reported feebleness, he described Roddy and Moody as "capable counsel, one of whom has enjoyed a long and successful practise before the courts of Jackson County."

Although the Supreme Court did not announce when it would issue its decision, a rumor circulated that it would rule on the case on Monday, November 7. With a gathering of demonstrators on the steps outside the Supreme Court, conservative justice George Sutherland read the court's opinion. He indicated that the court had restricted itself to one question: "Whether the defendants were in substance denied the right of counsel, and if so, whether such denial infringes [on] the due process clause of the Fourteenth Amendment." The Court, with only two judges dissenting, held that Judge Hawkins's appointment of the boys' defense counsel, Stephen Roddy and Milo Moody, had been entirely too casual. According to Justice Sutherland, "From the time of their arraignment until the beginning of their trial, when consultation, thoroughgoing investigation and preparation were vitally important, the defendants did not have the aid of counsel in any real sense." The highest court of the land reversed the lower courts' decisions, paving the way for new trials. The Ku Klux Klan in Birmingham responded to the court's opinion by way of paper pamphlets: "Negroes of Birmingham, the Ku Klux Klan is watching you. Tell the Communists [the ILD] to get out of town. They mean only trouble for you, for Alabama is a good place for good Negroes and a bad place for Negroes who believe in racial equality."

On death row, the Scottsboro Boys had been treated badly. They received mail, donations of money, and gifts from around the world, and the guards had a particular dislike for them because of it. They resented that the boys were able to buy special meals, candy, and cigarettes to help make their lives more bearable in prison, and took every opportunity to show their disapproval. The young men were kept in their cells most of the time and not allowed to use the exercise yard. The guards seemed to single them out for embarrassment. Clarence Norris wrote, "They made us parade buck naked from our cells to the bath twice a week. . . . This was special treatment just for us." Their stay of execution so Pollak could argue their case before the Supreme Court didn't help their situation. Norris recalled that two guards "came to my cell in the dead of night. They called me to the door. When I got there it was like lightning had struck me. I was hit in the head with a pair of brass knuckles. While I was down they worked on my body. They kicked me in the balls, chest, ribs, head and everywhere. They damn near killed me. They did the same to Haywood Patterson."

On November 8, however, the day after the Supreme Court's decision was announced, the scene at Kilby Prison was celebratory. "The boys shouted, they were so glad. Andy Wright, from his cell, read out loud that we fellows won a new trial," wrote Patterson. By this time, these young men had been imprisoned for almost two years, eight of the youths in cells just down the hall from Alabama's electric chair and one, Roy Wright, in jail in Birmingham.

n, DC, demonstrations in support of the Scottsboro
d near the US Supreme Court. In a case that became
well v. *Alabama*, the court, in a seven to two vote,
abama had failed to give the young men adequate
in the Scottsboro trials, a violation of the equal
use of the Fourteenth Amendment.

6

A NEW YEAR, A NEW TRIAL

As a new year dawned, the future looked brighter for the nine young men than it had in some time. Yet they were still in prison. Poet Langston Hughes visited the death house on January 24, 1933, during a trip to the nearby Tuskegee Institute, a school established in 1881 by Booker T. Washington to teach young Negro men the skills necessary to earn a living. A local minister had suggested that his poetry might help cheer the boys. Hughes wrote, "Over Alabama that winter lay the shadow of Scottsboro. . . . I went down the long corridor to the death house to read poetry to the Scottsboro boys. In their grilled cells in that square room with a steel door to the electric chair at one end, in their gray prison uniforms, the eight black boys sat or lay listlessly in their bunks and paid little attention to me. . . . Only one boy [Andy Wright] came up to the bars and shook hands with me." Hughes chose mostly humorous poems to read to them. "I did not know what to say that might be helpful," he explained. "So I said nothing . . . except my hope that their appeals would end well."

The new year also brought with it a change of scenery. The Scottsboro Boys were transferred to the Birmingham jail to await their new trials, which were set to begin on March 27, 1933. Earlier in March, Judge Hawkins had finally agreed to the ILD's request for a change of venue. The defense had hoped the new trials would be held in Birmingham. Instead, they would be held in Decatur, Alabama, about sixty-five miles west of Scottsboro, in Morgan County, along the Tennessee River. A new judge would preside.

Before being transferred to Birmingham, Olen Montgomery wrote to William L. Patterson, executive secretary of the ILD, to voice thanks. "Since the supreme court has granted we boys a new trial," he wrote, "I thank [*sic*] it is my rite to express my thanks [and] appreciation to the whole party for thair care of me and the wonderful and faithful struggle for my rites. I am so happy over it until I don't hardle know exactly how to thank them for thair kindness love of us poor ones. But I do appreciate it to the very highest respect. . . . I my self feels like I have been born again." Roy Wright followed Montgomery's letter with one of his own to the ILD executive secretary: "I am . . . glad to know you all have succeeded in having [a] trial in another place and at this trial I hope to prove my self not guilty of the crime charged against me."

William Patterson knew that a good defense wouldn't be enough to free the boys. This time their defense would have to be brilliant and, in George Chamlee's words, "prove beyond question the innocence of the defendants." Patterson turned to Samuel S. Leibowitz, a New Yorker who had become one of the country's leading criminal lawyers. Leibowitz believed in the law, in justice always prevailing. At a meeting, he told Patterson and Joseph Brodsky, the ILD's lead lawyer, "Gentlemen, no matter what the prejudice may be, there is a basic rock of decency in every individual which a little scratching on the surface of the rock will remove whatever superficial prejudice there may be." The ILD men thought he was being naïve. Brodsky said to him, "You will be a sadder but wiser man when you are finished. We have been down there and we know what we are talking about." Leibowitz insisted, "If it is justice that these black men be adjudged innocent . . . I cannot believe that the people of Alabama will be false

At Trial: Decatur

James Edwin Horton Jr., presiding judge

FOR THE PROSECUTION:

Thomas Knight Jr., attorney general of Alabama;
Wade Wright, Morgan County solicitor

FOR THE DEFENSE:

Samuel S. Leibowitz, New York criminal attorney;
Joseph R. Brodsky, lead attorney for the
International Labor Defense (ILD);
George W. Chamlee, attorney from Chattanooga,
Tennessee

WITNESSES FOR THE PROSECUTION:

Victoria Price, accuser; **Dr. R. R. Bridges**, Scottsboro
physician

WITNESSES FOR THE DEFENSE:

J. S. Benson, editor of Scottsboro's *Progressive Age*
newspaper; **John Sanford**, Scottsboro plasterer;
Dallas Ramsay, resident of Chattanooga;
Dr. E. E. Reisman, Chattanooga gynecologist;
Percy Ricks, fireman on the freight train;
Haywood Patterson, the accused; **Lester Carter**, one
of the white hoboes aboard the train; **Ruby Bates**

to their great heritage of honor, and to those brave and chivalrous generations of the past, in whose blood the history of their State is written." The ILD couldn't afford Leibowitz, but he agreed to take the case for no fee if the ILD renounced any communist connection and gave him complete control of the defense. William Patterson and Brodsky agreed.

Leibowitz planned to ask that the original charges be quashed, or thrown out, because the nine youths' constitutional rights had been violated. By excluding members of the boys' own race from the jury lists in 1931, the Jackson County court in Scottsboro had denied them a trial before their peers, as guaranteed by the equal protection clause of the Fourteenth Amendment. A believer in showing rather than telling, in demonstrating rather than discussing, Leibowitz subpoenaed the jury commissioners from Jackson County and their jury rolls. He also planned to put qualified Negro citizens on the stand in an attempt to establish that they had been denied jury duty purely because of the color of their skin. He realized his strategy was not a guarantee of success, but if it failed and the case moved forward to trial, it would at least leave open a door for a future appeal. Also, if his move to toss out the charges failed, he was ready to present a strong defense of the nine youths.

Leibowitz worked with Joseph Brodsky and George Chamlee to collect evidence against the two accusers, Victoria Price and Ruby Bates. As Clarence Norris told the story, "They got depositions and affidavits from people who swore the women were prostitutes. They found Lester Carter, one of the white boys we threw off the train. He swore he and another boy had sex with Victoria and Ruby in a hobo jungle the night before our arrest. He said Orville Gilley, the white boy we let stay on the train, had told him nobody had raped those girls." Leibowitz went so far as to have a model of the train made.

Attorney General Thomas Knight would prosecute the case for

the state. Knight was less concerned about the jury issue than he was about the disappearance of one of his main witnesses. Knight argued that the selection of potential jurors was entirely up to the jury commissioners and a matter of states' rights. He saw nothing wrong with the nature of the Scottsboro juries. Knight's real concern was that Ruby Bates had disappeared from her home in Huntsville on February 28. Bates had been a disappointing witness for the prosecution from the beginning. She had not been as forthcoming or as convincing as Victoria Price. She had been reluctant to identify which, if any, of the boys had raped her and Price, and she had hinted after the first trials that she had information that might help the defense. Even so, she was one of the accusers and now she was missing. The attorney general was so fearful of losing his "remaining star witness . . . that a deputy sheriff [was] assigned to watch night and day at the barely furnished little shack where" Price lived. Adding to Knight's worries was a letter Bates had written to Earl Streetman, a boyfriend, in which she claimed the girls' accusations were lies. In the letter Bates wrote, "Those police man made me tell a lie. . . . those negros did not touch me. . . . i wish those negroes are not burnt on account of me." The letter came to light when the Huntsville police arrested an ex-fighter for public drunkenness and searched him. Bates had given him the letter to deliver to Streetman.

Before the March trials began, the boys were transferred again, this time from Birmingham to the Decatur jail. Recalling their new accommodations, Norris wrote:

> The Decatur jail was a hellhole. It was declared
> unfit for white prisoners over a year before we got
> there. . . . It was filthy, dust everywhere, big holes
> were in the floors and walls, plaster fell down
> around our heads, the stink was sickening and rats

the size of rabbits had the run of the place. But
the bedbugs! There were millions of them, large
as grains of rice. They crawled all over us at night
and sleep was hard to come by. . . . We raised hell
about these bugs and they gave us some powder
to kill them. But they just ate that stuff and came
back for more.

When the trials began on Monday, March 27 they were held in
the courtroom of Judge James Edwin Horton Jr. The case against
Haywood Patterson was the first to be heard.

Leibowitz opened, as he had planned, with a motion to quash
the original indictments against the boys "on the ground that
Negroes were excluded from the grand jury." *New York Times* reporter
F. Raymond Daniell explained, "The South's traditional attitude
toward the Negro—an attitude of benevolent paternalism[—] . . .
refuses . . . to recognize the equal rights guaranteed by the Fourteenth
Amendment." Leibowitz accused the state of systematically
excluding blacks from jury pools and urged Judge Horton to uphold
the Fourteenth Amendment to the Constitution. Knight objected to
Leibowitz's portrayal of Alabama and challenged the New Yorker to
prove it.

That was what Leibowitz planned to do over the course of the
next several days. He called J. S. Benson, the editor of Scottsboro's
Progressive Age newspaper, to testify. Although Benson was an unwilling
witness for the defense, he had observed the Scottsboro court almost
daily for close to thirty years. He admitted that he'd never known of
a black person serving on a jury there. When it was his turn to cross-
examine the witness, Attorney General Knight read the Alabama
jury statute aloud, which said prospective jurors had to be of good
character, judgment, and intelligence, and also owners of property.

Benson told the attorney general, "I know some good Negroes as far as Negroes go. But I think that sound judgment part of the statute—I think they can't get around that." When Leibowitz asked the editor what he meant by sound judgment, Benson said, "They're not trained, you know, and I might say the same applies to women." As Leibowitz pursued his questioning, Benson finally said, "They'll all steal."

Leibowitz then called two Jackson County jury commissioners. Like Benson before them, they were reluctant witnesses. While neither of them could say one way or the other whether the names on the jury lists were those of blacks or whites, they also confessed that they couldn't recall a Negro actually ever serving on a jury. According to Knight, the names on the lists were not a matter of "exclusion," but rather of "selection." But Alabama had a long history of exclusion. When delegates met to write the state's constitution in 1901, "the political leaders of Alabama had bluntly stated their goal: 'to secure permanent white supremacy in this State.'"

Before the end of the first day, Leibowitz called John Sanford to the stand. He was a Negro plasterer in Scottsboro, and he named several members of his church who he believed fit the requirements to be jurors. His testimony went smoothly, until the next day, when fireworks erupted. At Tuesday's cross-examination, Knight got up close to Sanford, pointed his finger in the witness's face, and spoke in a loud, aggressive voice. The prosecuting attorney was surprised and agitated when Leibowitz objected, yelling, "You are not going to bully this witness or any other witness." Knight stepped back, but he resumed his questions. Attempting to demonstrate that Sanford lacked the intelligence to sit on a jury, he asked, referring to a word that had come up earlier, "And you don't know what the word esteemed means, John?" Again, Leibowitz interrupted, saying, "Call him Mr. Sanford, please." Knight was shaken, saying, "I'm not accustomed to that."

In all, Leibowitz called to the witness chair nine members of Scottsboro's black community, each of whom was qualified to be a juror under the Alabama state statute. Yet, not one had ever been called to jury service. Knight abruptly changed his argument from there being no qualified Negroes to serve on a jury to insisting that Leibowitz had not proven there were no black names included on the jury rolls. Leibowitz responded by threatening to bring in every man on the lists to prove all were white.

In the end, Judge Horton denied the motion to quash the indictments against the nine youths. Leibowitz wasn't surprised by this, but he wanted his arguments in the court record for later appeal. Horton announced a one-day adjournment.

When the trial resumed on Thursday, Leibowitz continued his argument that the jury system in Alabama was rigged and in violation of the Fourteenth Amendment. Leaving Jackson County behind, he turned his attention to Morgan County, where Decatur was located. He called one of the county's three jury commissioners to the stand and, over Knight's objections, demanded the leather-bound book that contained the names of potential jurors. Morgan County had a much larger black middle class than did Jackson County, and many were college educated. Yet the names of black citizens were absent from the jury pool. To strengthen his argument, Leibowitz called several leading members of Morgan County's black community. None had ever been called to jury service. They testified at some risk to their personal safety. After appearing on the witness stand, dentist Frank Sykes was so harassed by Decatur's white citizens he felt the need to leave the city and spent the rest of his life in Baltimore, Maryland. Surprising Leibowitz, Judge Horton abruptly admitted that the defense attorney had made his point. But he also ruled that the trial would continue.

During that first week of Patterson's new trial, Leibowitz's fight against the Alabama jury-selection process antagonized some of the spectators who filled the court. They were unaccustomed to having their state's legal procedures questioned and to seeing the truthfulness of white witnesses challenged. Some whispered threats against the New York lawyer. Captain Joseph Burleson, commander of the thirty National Guardsmen sent to Decatur to protect the nine defendants and to maintain order, had heard the whispers and worried about Leibowitz's safety. As a precaution, he stationed five guardsmen outside the apartment where Leibowitz and his wife were staying. Others, especially those who believed in the innocence of the nine young men, were concerned that Leibowitz's attack on Alabama's judicial process had already lost him the case.

By the time Leibowitz wrapped up his Fourteenth Amendment arguments, it was shortly before noon on Friday, March 31. Before adjourning for the weekend and even before jurors had been chosen for the Haywood Patterson trial, Judge Horton addressed the courtroom. "Now gentlemen," he said,

> under our law when it comes to the courts we know neither native or alien, we know neither Jew nor Gentile, we know neither black nor white, native or foreign born, but to each it is our duty to mete out even handed justice. . . . [But I] must tell you that it is the duty of all citizens here, no matter who they are, no matter what their creed or race is, no matter whether white or back [sic] to calmly abide by the decisions of your courts. There is no other way of enjoying the fruits of liberty, except by following out the law as laid down to you, and obeying the law as it is.

When the trial resumed on Monday morning, April 3, Attorney General Knight called the star witness for the state. Taking only "twelve minutes of the court's time," Victoria Price smoothly repeated her testimony from the Scottsboro trials—describing how she and Bates had traveled to Chattanooga, stayed with Mrs. Callie Brochie, looked for work in the mills, and caught the return train. Then, thrusting her finger at Haywood Patterson, she "unhesitatingly" identified him "as one of six Negroes who . . . had attacked her." There was little that was new to her story. But Knight surprised the courtroom when he reached into his briefcase on the prosecution's table and pulled out a torn pair of underpants. Showing them to Price, he fired off several questions: "Are those the step-ins you had on . . .?" "Have they been in your care since [the attack] happened?" "Are they now in the same condition as they were, just as they were pulled off of you?" Price answered yes to each, and Knight offered the underwear to the court as evidence. Leibowitz jumped to his feet, saying, "This is the first time in two years any such step-ins have ever been shown in any court of justice. They were not produced at the first trial or second trial or any of the four trials at Scottsboro. This is the first time in two year [sic] any step-ins have been produced in any court." According to Patterson, Knight "picked them up and said, 'Well, they're here now,' and he tossed them plonk into the face of one of the jurors." The courtroom erupted in laughter. Judge Horton cautioned the spectators that he would "not permit any disorder," but he allowed the underwear as evidence.

Leibowitz tried to open his cross-examination of Price with a discussion of where on the train the alleged assault had happened as it rumbled toward Paint Rock from Chattanooga. For that purpose, he had had the Lionel Corporation, which produced model trains, construct a replica of the freight train the two accusers and the nine

Leibowitz commissioned a model train to be built to help with the defense, but Price refused to acknowledge that it exactly represented the train upon which she had ridden. Yet the train's conductor said it was indeed in the same configuration as the real train.

accused had ridden that Wednesday in March 1931. It was set up in the exact configuration as the real train. Leibowitz quickly got a taste of how difficult the prosecution's star witness was going to be. Pointing to the model, he asked, "That is a fairly good representation of the box car you were in?" Her response was unexpected. "I won't go by that box car," she said. He tried to pin her down by asking her to say how the replica was different. She answered, "Because that is not the train I was on." Growing weary, Leibowitz rephrased his question: "Of course you were not on this minature [*sic*] train, I asked you if this is a fair representation?" Finally, she agreed that it was "kinda a little bit" like the boxcar she had been on, but the real train "was bigger, lots bigger, that is a toy."

Leibowitz then questioned the woman about her past. Had she ever been arrested for lewdness and adultery? Had she ever been convicted of any crime? Had she not broken up a home by seeing a married man? Price denied these accusations, suggesting it was probably somebody else who was also named Victoria Price. He cast doubt on the extent of the injuries she said she'd received during the alleged assault on the train. Six men, she claimed, violently raped her while she struggled atop a bed of sharp gravel. Where were the bruises? Another man, according to her story, struck her in the head with the butt end of a pistol, causing a bloody gash. Why didn't the doctors who examined her in Scottsboro include this in their reports? To support his claim that Price was an untrustworthy witness, Leibowitz offered the court "certified copies of court records from Huntsville." These records showed that Price "had been arrested for offenses against the moral code." Judge Horton rejected them, as they were infractions of Huntsville's city, or municipal, codes rather than Alabama state laws. Violations of municipal codes were not admissible as evidence in state trials.

Throughout his cross-examination, Leibowitz had been exasperated by the witness. At times he roared at her and argued with her, and Price shouted back to the point that one observer thought she might strike him. In the eyes of most Southerners, calling into question the honesty and integrity of a white woman, no matter how poor she was or what her circumstances, was deplorable. Determined to make a point, recalling Price's testimony about Mrs. Callie Brochie, Leibowitz said, in a casual way, "By the way Mrs. Price, as a matter of fact the name of Mrs. Callie you apply to this boardin [*sic*] house lady, is the name of a boarding house lady used by Octavius Roy Cohn in [his stories in] the *Saturday Evening Post* . . . Sis Callie, isn't that where you got the name?" His goal met, he returned to his seat at the defense table, even as the attorney general leaped to his feet to protest.

Some of the all-white, all-male jurors from Morgan County chosen [i]n the 1933 retrial of Haywood Patterson. Note the model train in

The final witness that Monday was one of the two doctors who examined Price and Bates in Scottsboro within an hour and a half of the supposed assault. Called by Knight, Dr. R. R. Bridges repeated the same findings he'd reported at the Scottsboro trials. His testimony there had been crucial to the prosecution's case and had not been adequately, if at all, challenged by Stephen Roddy. Leibowitz, however, turned the state's witness into one for the defense when he got the doctor to acknowledge that neither woman exhibited signs of a violent struggle or of rape. The spermatozoa Dr. Bridges had found during his examination of Price were nonmotile, or dead. This was a remarkable revelation: Price had claimed she had been raped by six men, but there was no medical evidence to support that.

Dr. Marvin Lynch, the second Scottsboro physician who examined the women, was scheduled to take the witness chair the next day. He never took the stand, however, because Attorney General Knight wished him excused. His testimony, Knight explained to Judge Horton, would be a repetition of that of Dr. Bridges. The judge agreed to Knight's request. Lynch then met briefly with Horton to say his testimony would not be the same because he was convinced the women were lying. Horton urged him to testify, but Lynch said that, despite wanting to, he couldn't. If he testified for the defense he'd never be able to show his face in Scottsboro again. Nearly thirty-five years later, in October 1967, Lynch denied he'd ever told Horton he thought the women were lying.

When Leibowitz called the first witness for the defense, he summoned Dallas Ramsay to the stand. Ramsay was a Negro, and he testified that he saw Price "with a white youth in the 'hobo jungle' alongside the railroad yard in Chattanooga, on the morning of the day" of the supposed crime. Only the day before, Price claimed that she and Bates had been alone and had never visited the hobo jungle. Attorney General Knight objected to the testimony, as he did to almost every question Leibowitz asked of this witness and others he would call to testify. He asked Leibowitz how Ramsay's statement was relevant to the case. Leibowitz answered, "I'm going to show that the State's main witness is a perjurer. That's what I'm going to show before I'm through. This is only the beginning." Horton allowed Ramsay's statement into the record.

In addition to calling the other defendants to testify in the Patterson trial, Leibowitz called people from Chattanooga who knew Price and Bates. These witnesses addressed the women's characters. He called a Chattanooga gynecologist, Dr. E. E. Reisman, who explained that "the Price woman's story of the attack contained biological inconsistencies." According to Reisman, the medical testimony offered by the two doctors who examined Price in Scottsboro "was sufficient . . . to make a man of science skeptical about Mrs. Price's statement that she was attacked by six Negroes." Another witness, Percy Ricks, who was the fireman of the freight train on which Price had ridden, said that when the train pulled into Paint Rock, "the two women seemed just as anxious to get away as the Negroes." He described the scene: "I saw them both running up toward the engine. Some of the men with shotguns [the posse] came around and headed them off. Then they turned and ran the other way until another batch of men came up from that direction and stopped them."

When Patterson took the stand in his own defense, he told Leibowitz that he had not seen any girls on the train. He confessed to fighting with the white boys, but the first he knew about the two female hoboes was when he saw them in Paint Rock. Perhaps it was a way to trip up a witness, but on cross-examination Knight asked Patterson if he'd been "tried at Scottsboro."

Patterson's response surprised the prosecuting attorney. "No, sir," he answered. "I was framed at Scottsboro."

"Who told you to say that?" Knight demanded, shouting.

As Dr. R. R. Bridges testifies in the April 1933 trial in Decatur, Alabama, Judge James E. Horton leans over to listen to what the witness is saying. Bridges was originally a witness for the state, or prosecution, but the defendants' attorney Samuel Leibowitz realized the doctor's medical testimony could be used to bolster

"I told myself to say it."

Despite Knight's attempts to shake his story, Patterson continued to deny any knowledge of Price and Bates until Paint Rock. He denied that he'd touched them in any way.

During these first few days of the trial, Leibowitz had received a number of threatening letters. Many local townsfolk not only resented the way he challenged Alabama's jury process, they also objected to his treatment of Price. There were rumblings around town "that a mob was plotting to lynch the nine Negro prisoners lodged in the rickety old jail and run Samuel S. Leibowitz . . . out of town." Leibowitz dismissed the threats, but Judge Horton, on hearing about them, did not. As the trial resumed after lunch that Wednesday, he said, "The court wishes to make an announcement." He warned the spectators in the room that the purpose of the trial was to find the truth. "If these defendants are guilty they should be punished. If they are not guilty, they should be acquitted. That is for the court and the jury to determine. . . . I have no tolerance for mob spirit." And then, in a stern voice, he warned that anyone who attempted to take the lives of the prisoners or interfere with any other person connected with the trial "may expect to forfeit his life."

If Knight had stunned the defense by pulling Price's torn underwear out of his briefcase, what happened on Thursday caused the prosecution considerable distress. Leibowitz called his first surprise witness, Lester Carter. Carter was one of the white boys who had been aboard the train when the fight broke out with Patterson and the other black youths. He readily admitted that when he calculated the odds of overcoming the black youths, his courage had failed him, and he had gone over the side of the train.

Although Price, in her previous testimony, had claimed that she and Bates had gone to Chattanooga and returned on the Huntsville-bound train alone, Carter said this wasn't true. He claimed he'd met

Lester Carter, who had been on the train with the Scottsboro Boys,

Price and her boyfriend, L. J. "Jack" Tiller, while he was in jail for vagrancy. Price and Tiller were also in jail and serving a sentence for adultery. Tiller was a married man. The first night out of jail, the three met up in Huntsville at Price's house, where Price promised to introduce Carter to her friend Ruby Bates. The next night, March 23, 1931, the four spent the night in Huntsville's hobo camp, where each couple, lying in a bed of honeysuckle less than three feet from the other, had engaged in physical relations multiple times. They plotted then to meet and ride the rails to Chattanooga the next afternoon, but Tiller begged off, not wanting another arrest for adultery.

Now a trio, Carter, Price, and Bates met up as planned and took the train to Chattanooga, where they made a new friend, Orville Gilley. Not having any money for lodging, the four spent the night sleeping along the railroad tracks in Chattanooga, where, according to Carter, he and Bates had physical relations again. The next morning they returned aboard the Huntsville-bound train.

Morgan County solicitor Wade Wright, acting as an assistant to Knight, tried to shake Carter's testimony on cross-examination. But Carter stuck to his story. Yet Wright won points with the jury when he got the young drifter to admit that the ILD's Joseph Brodsky had paid his room and board in Decatur and even bought him a new suit.

Carter, however, was just a warm-up act. Leibowitz's main surprise was revealed shortly after noon. In a carefully staged entrance, he called the previously missing Ruby Bates to the stand. There was an audible gasp from the spectators. Even "Judge Horton left the bench and stood in the railed enclosure as every one turned and looked at the single entrance to the court room." Flanked by National Guardsmen with bayonets fixed to their weapons, Bates walked slowly through the door. Confusion and worry swept over the faces of those sitting at the prosecution table.

Leibowitz asked to have Price brought in from a waiting room

Ruby Bates, Leibowitz's surprise witness in 1933, takes the stand to recant her accusations of rape, explaining that Victoria Price had concocted the story so the two women would not be sent to adjacent to the courtroom so Bates could identify her. F. Raymond Daniell, in Decatur to report on the trial, described their meeting: "Mrs. Price was panting with anger and excitement. Attorney General Knight edged his way in between the two women and cautioned the State's main witness to 'keep your temper.'" Price was taken back out of the courtroom, and Leibowitz began his questioning of Bates.

Bates's testimony confirmed Lester Carter's sworn statements. When asked where she had gone, she explained that she'd gone to New York, where she met with the Reverend Dr. Harry Emerson Fosdick. About their meeting, when interviewed later by a reporter, Fosdick said, "She came alone and of her own free will." He described their meeting as a "confessional," and he advised her to return to Alabama and "tell the truth." When Knight challenged Bates with her testimony from the Scottsboro trials, she said, "I told it just like Victoria did because she said we might have to stay in jail if we did not frame up a story after crossing a State line with men."

In his closing argument, Leibowitz appealed to the jurors' sense of logic. He asked them to weigh the evidence and testimony and to realize that reasonable doubt existed as to Patterson's guilt. Based on Wade Wright's attack on the ILD during his cross-examination of Carter and the general anti-Jewish and anti–New York sentiment in Alabama, Leibowitz feared that the prosecution's closing statement might try to focus the jury's attention on him, a Jewish New Yorker, rather than on the facts of the case. Leibowitz felt that he needed to add that he wasn't accepting any fees and that he wasn't a crusader for Negro social equality. He was there, he said, to see that justice was done and "to see that the law guaranteeing equal protection to all races in our courts is observed."

Leibowitz was right about the prosecution's closing statement. Wade Wright, for the state of Alabama, appealed both to state pride and prejudice. He urged jurors to "show them, show them that

Alabama justice cannot be bought and sold with Jew money from New York." He ripped into Bates's fine New York clothing, which she wore to court upon her return to Alabama, and commented, "Don't you know these people, these defense witnesses, are bought and paid for?"

When he handed the case to the jury at around one o'clock on Saturday afternoon, Judge Horton advised the jurors: "You are not trying whether or not the defendant is white or black . . . you are trying whether or not this defendant forcibly ravished a woman. You are not trying lawyers, you are not trying State lines; but you are here . . . to see justice done in this case." The next day was Palm Sunday, and the jury returned its verdict that morning shortly before eleven: guilty. For the second time, a white male jury sentenced Haywood Patterson to die in Alabama's electric chair. Although he wasn't the only Negro in the court that day, Patterson said about the verdict: "The sun came in the [courtroom] windows strong and made everything that was white look whiter, and me the one thing black, I guess, look blacker."

After all was said and done, Leibowitz walked to the bench and extended his hand. Judge Horton took it, and the two men shook hands warmly. Leibowitz had been impressed with the way the judge had attempted to hold a trial free from prejudice. "I am taking back to New York with me a picture of one of the finest jurists I have ever met," said Leibowitz. "But I am sorry I cannot say as much for a jury which has decided this case against the weight of evidence." He called their verdict "an act of bigots spitting on the tomb of the immortal Abraham Lincoln." Later, the New York lawyer issued a formal statement in which he called the decision "a mockery of justice" and "a piece of judicial lynching."

On Monday, April 17, 1933, eight days after the jury had returned its ruling, Haywood Patterson stood before Judge Horton for the official sentencing. The judge asked Patterson if he had anything to say. Patterson mumbled, "I ain't had a fair trial. Ain't seen no girls on that train. I ain't had a fair trial." Judge Horton set Patterson's date of execution for June 16 at Kilby Prison. But as soon as he had set the date, he suspended it, in response to a motion for a new trial by Joseph Brodsky. Judge Horton then postponed the dates of the remaining trials until "the passions of local citizens had subsided."

Throughout the remainder of April and May, Judge Horton thought about the Scottsboro cases. He had questions about the truthfulness of the state's main witness. He even suggested to Attorney General Knight that he dismiss the cases against those not yet tried and pardon Patterson, but Knight had higher political ambitions and realized such a move would be career suicide in Alabama. He was committed to the prosecution of the Scottsboro Boys.

On June 22, Judge Horton convened court to hear arguments for a new Patterson trial. He listened to the evidence and then read a lengthy prepared statement concerning the Scottsboro cases. He concluded:

> History, sacred and profane, and the common experience of mankind teaches us that women of the character shown in this case are prone for selfish reasons to make false accusations both of rape and of insult upon the slightest provocation, or even without provocation for ulterior purposes. . . .
>
> This tendency on the part of the women shows that they are pre-disposed to make false accusations upon any occasion whereby their selfish ends may be gained.
>
> The Court will not pursue the evidence any further.

Outside the courtroom, Haywood Patterson kisses his mother at

As heretofore stated the law declares that
a defendant should not be convicted without
corroboration where the testimony of the prosecutrix
[female accuser] bears on its face indications of
unreliability or improbability and particularly when
it is contradicted by other evidence.

The testimony of the prosecutrix [Victoria Price]
in this case is not only uncorroborated, but it also
bears on its face indications of improbability and
is contradicted by other evidence, and in addition
thereto the evidence greatly preponderates in favor
of the defendant. It therefore becomes the duty of
the Court under the law to grant the motion made
in this case.

The verdict and sentence against Haywood Patterson were set aside. He would get another trial.

Judge Horton hoped his decision would permanently end the prosecution of the Scottsboro cases, but Knight vowed to continue. In 1934, Knight was elected lieutenant governor of Alabama. But the people of Alabama "got sore as hell at Judge Horton," Patterson wrote later. In the May primary leading up to that election, despite vigorous campaigning on his part, Horton lost his judgeship and returned to private life.

7

BEFORE JUDGE CALLAHAN

William Washington Callahan, who replaced Judge Horton on the bench in the Scottsboro cases, was a no-nonsense judge. He had no formal education in the law. Instead, he received his training by reading books and from working as a clerk in a law office. He was seventy years of age when he stepped into the Scottsboro trials in November 1933. Haywood Patterson described him as "the toughest, most freckle-faced, bald-headed man I was ever up against." Clarence Norris seemed to share that view. He later wrote that Callahan "was a redneck from the word go. His robes might as well have been those of the Ku Klux Klan."

Patterson's retrial opened with two days of hearings devoted to a motion for a change of venue. Leibowitz's argument was that Patterson's previous trial had been so well publicized locally that it would be difficult to find an impartial jury. Callahan denied the motion. He believed the state had spent enough money trying Patterson and the other defendants. According to Norris, Judge Callahan "wanted to get the trials over with as fast as he could." He was in such a rush to conclude this episode in Alabama history that "reporters nicknamed him 'Speedy' Callahan."

After the judge dismissed the motion for a change of venue, Leibowitz once again raised the issue of the juries. To prove that

Both to prevent escape and to protect the defendants, armed guards escorted the young men between the jail and the Morgan County courthouse throughout their trials in Decatur.

blacks were systematically excluded from jury rolls, he asked that the lists from Jackson County, where the Scottsboro trials were first held, be brought into court. J. E. Moody, who was head of the Jackson County jury commission, took the stand with the large, leather-bound volume containing the names of citizens qualified to serve on juries. Leibowitz asked him to read the names and to identify the race of each. Moody read for a full hour without turning up the name of a single black person. C. A. Wann, the court clerk, then took over reading the names in the book. He read and read, until shortly after four o'clock that afternoon, when he read the name of one black man. After several more hours of testimony, he uncovered the names of others. These names had been squeezed onto the pages in the ledger. Although surprised, Leibowitz remained unflappable.

When court resumed on Saturday, he was ready with a hand-writing expert. Leibowitz charged that "the jury roll was forged after indictment of the [nine] Negroes [in 1931] and after [his] criticism of the Alabama jury system." The expert determined that Leibowitz's suspicions were valid: the jury rolls had been tampered with; the names of Negroes had been added after March 1931. The defense asked again that the original indictments against the boys be dropped, but Judge Callahan denied that request. The judge refused to question "the honesty of the sworn officials of Jackson County without more substantial evidence." Judge Callahan was annoyed that the trial thus far was taking so long. He called Leibowitz to the bench and said, "We're going to make speed beginning Monday." Although Patterson's trial before Judge Horton had taken a week, Judge Callahan wanted the retrial to be done within three days.

After the Patterson jury was selected, Judge Callahan kept rushing the trial toward its conclusion. As Leibowitz assembled his toy freight train in court on Monday, November 27, Judge Callahan began fidgeting on the bench and looking at his watch. He didn't understand the purpose of Leibowitz's model. He protested that everyone knew "the difference between engines, box cars and cabooses." When Leibowitz said he was almost finished, the judge told the attorney a "few more flicks and frills may be all right." Then, just as quickly, he sniped, "I hope you'll get this done before Christmas because Santa Claus is going to get all that anyway."

He often interrupted Leibowitz with a "hurry it along" or "that's enough on that" when the defense lawyer lingered too long, in the judge's estimation, on a subject. When the defense lawyer questioned Victoria Price, who had taken the stand to repeat her story, Judge Callahan cautioned the attorney to "treat the lady with more respect." He wouldn't allow Leibowitz to ask her questions about her relationships with Jack Tiller or Orville Gilley. Off-limits, too, were questions about Ruby Bates, Lester Carter, and Chattanooga's hobo jungle. When Leibowitz asked Price if she had ever been convicted of lewdness, the judge objected even before the prosecution could and wouldn't allow the witness to answer. The judge's refusal to allow an investigation into Price's character or her movements before and during the trip to Chattanooga crippled the defense.

Orville Gilley took the stand, and his testimony once again supported Price's story. But almost every time Leibowitz asked a question of the vagabond and the prosecution objected, the judge routinely upheld the objection. At one point, Leibowitz protested, saying, "But, Your Honor, won't you excuse the jury and allow me to inform you of what I am trying to prove?" The judge's response was curt and to the point. "I can imagine," he said, and ordered the defense attorney to move on to something else. Yet, when Leibowitz voiced objections to the prosecution's line of questioning, Judge Callahan often overruled them.

Ruby Bates did not take the stand at this trial. Early in November she had returned to New York. Since appearing in Decatur before

Judge Horton's court, she had received numerous threats and feared for her life. The defense was set to have her respond to questions in a sworn, written statement, but Callahan would have none of it. He ruled they would go on with the trial without Bates's deposition. Nor would he hold up the proceedings for medical experts Leibowitz planned to call from Chattanooga that would support the defense's claim that the boys were innocent.

When Patterson took the stand in his own defense, Leibowitz tried to lessen the impact of the damaging testimony the defendant had given in Scottsboro, when he had claimed that everyone but himself, Eugene Williams, and the Wright brothers had attacked the girls. By way of explanation, Patterson said he "disremembered" the events of March 25, 1931. He went on to add, "We was scared and I don't know what I said. They told us if we didn't confess they'd kill us—give us to the mob outside. . . . And Mr. Bailey [the circuit solicitor, part of the prosecution team] over there—he said send all the niggers to the electric chair. There's too many niggers in the world, anyway." While Judge Callahan had not allowed the women's reputations or their activities in the days and hours before the alleged attack to be discussed, he ruled that Patterson's previous testimony in Scottsboro should stand.

With the defense strategy severely handicapped by the judge's rulings, Leibowitz attacked the prosecution. At this trial, Knight had not bothered to call the physicians who had examined Price and Bates upon their arrival in Scottsboro. He believed Dr. Bridges's testimony in the Patterson trial before Judge Horton, in which the doctor said there were no signs of rape, could have lost him the case. Knight wouldn't risk having his own witness being turned against him again. Pointing all this out to the jury, Leibowitz asked, "What do you think of a prosecution which hides evidence like that?" He said the state's case against Patterson and the others was "rotten from start to finish."

For Knight's part, he appealed to the jurors' "passion for protecting the womanhood of the State of Alabama. . . . If you believe this defendant raped Victoria Price, be men enough to return such a verdict as you know and I know will be a deterrent to others."

On November 30, Judge Callahan wrapped up the trial, reminding the twelve men in the jury box that the law "guarantees . . . [Patterson] a fair, just and impartial hearing and determination as to his guilt or his innocence. . . . The most humble, the most despised, the most abandoned, the confirmed criminal, as to that matter, comes into court with that guarantee." Before giving the case to the jury to weigh the evidence and arrive at a verdict, however, he contradicted Judge Horton's notion about corroboration: "The law would authorize a conviction on the testimony of Victoria Price alone. . . . The law does not require corroboration." Price's testimony was all that was required for a guilty verdict. Judge Callahan ended his instructions, saying, "Take the case, gentlemen, and give it your consideration."

Leibowitz rushed to the bench. Attorney General Knight followed him. In a brief and whispered conference, Leibowitz reminded the judge that he'd not mentioned anything about acquittal, or finding Patterson innocent. Somewhat embarrassed at this oversight, the judge added, "I believe I overlooked one thing. . . . If after considering all the evidence in this case you are not satisfied beyond all reasonable doubt that the defendant is guilty as charged, then he ought to be acquitted and must be under the law."

The next afternoon, even as the jury in the case against Clarence Norris was being sworn in, a deputy sheriff raced to the jail to get Patterson. His jury was ready to announce its verdict. The case ended as had Patterson's first and second trials. John Green, the court clerk, read it: "We find the defendant guilty as charged in the indictment and fix his punishment at death." The jury had reached its unanimous decision almost as soon as it left the courtroom to deliberate. It decided to believe Price's word over Patterson's denial. But it spent the next eleven and a half hours discussing his sentence. The jurors had been divided nine to three on his punishment—the majority wanted the electric chair, while the others sought life in prison. When the judge passed sentence on him later, Patterson "noticed he left out the Lord." Instead of asking the Lord to show Patterson mercy, which would have been customary, the judge "didn't even want the Lord to have any mercy on me."

Surprisingly, some of the Alabama newspapers began to question the verdict and even the trial itself, calling into doubt Price's truthfulness. The *Birmingham Post* ran an editorial called "A Questionable Trial." It read, in part, "The record of this trial, when it comes to review by the United States Supreme Court, will not be a favorable commentary on Alabama judicial procedure." In New York, Ruby Bates heard about Patterson's guilty verdict. She responded, "He's not guilty. Why should he be punished for something he's not guilty of? I never saw any of those boys until I went to Scottsboro. That's the only time I saw Heywood [*sic*] Patterson. I hope they all go free."

Clarence Norris's trial was a repeat of the Patterson trial. After a prolonged deliberation in which the jury could not settle on electrocution or life in prison, the defense grew optimistic for an acquittal. Their optimism was fleeting. When the verdict was read, Norris, too, was found guilty and the punishment was set at death. Judge Callahan ordered that both Norris and Patterson be put to death on February 2, 1934. Within an hour, Leibowitz had filed a notice that he planned to appeal, which automatically postponed their date of execution.

The atmosphere in the courtroom that Wednesday, December 6, when the Norris verdict was read, was tense. Leibowitz asked Callahan if he could leave immediately after the sentence was

After reversing her testimony that she had been assaulted, Ruby Bates spoke at ILD rallies and joined marches, like this one in Washington, DC, in an effort to free the young men.

imposed. The defense attorney "had been warned . . . that several men in the court room were waiting with loaded guns for him to leave the building." Leibowitz was escorted out of the courthouse by armed guards, one a former New York state trooper and the other from New York's homicide squad. They, along with three Alabama deputies, accompanied Leibowitz and New York news reporters past the Alabama state line to Chattanooga, Tennessee, where they caught a train bound for New York.

In February 1934, Leibowitz received a jolt when he learned that the papers for Patterson's appeal to the state supreme court had not been filed in time. Whether it was ignorance of the law or trickery aimed to guarantee that Patterson lingered in jail, Judge Callahan had granted the defense additional time to file for Patterson's appeal. Although Attorney General Knight had not objected, the judge had overstepped his authority in granting the extension, because it contradicted state law. When the Patterson and Norris cases reached the Alabama Supreme Court, Leibowitz once again argued the jury issue. Knight insisted that Patterson's appeal shouldn't even be considered because the defense lawyers had not filed the documents in time. He maintained that if the court ruled in the defense's favor over the issue of the juries, the court would be substituting itself for the "the jury commission" in every county in Alabama. In other words, it would be overstepping its legal authority. When the court's decision was delivered on June 28, 1934, it unanimously denied the motion for new trials for both defendants. Patterson's appeal was set aside on the grounds that the paperwork "had not been filed within ninety days after the final judgment by the trial court." In the Norris case, the court rejected the notion that blacks were systematically excluded from the Jackson County and Morgan County jury lists.

Even as the defense was filing appeals with the US Supreme Court, other troubles were brewing as 1934 came to a close. As early as May 1933, Victoria Price had told George W. Chamlee that she would be willing to change her story for the right price. Although nothing came of that conversation, J. T. Pearson, a man from Birmingham, wrote to the ILD in June 1934 and suggested that Price would change her story if "properly rewarded."

The ILD's Joseph Brodsky selected Samuel Schriftman, a New York attorney, to meet with Price. While negotiating with the woman, Schriftman used the name "Daniel Swift." Meanwhile, Price decided to double-cross the ILD. She told the Huntsville police that the ILD had first offered her $500 to change her story. By September, she said, "the offer had been increased to $1,000." The police urged her to play along. She agreed to meet with Schriftman and a Brodsky associate, Sol Kone, on October 1 in Nashville, Tennessee. Instead of witnessing Price sign an affidavit withdrawing her accusations, both men, along with J. T. Pearson, were arrested on the charge of bribery. In Schriftman's car the arresting officers found fifteen hundred one-dollar bills. Schriftman denied it was his. The men each posted a $500 bond but forfeited it when they failed to show up in court. No arrest warrants were ever issued.

When Leibowitz found out about the ILD's bribery attempt, he was outraged. He believed in the boys' innocence and released a statement that said, "I knew nothing of the activities of the two men from the International Labor Defense who were arrested in Nashville, charged with attempting to bribe Victoria Price. The defense needed no such help. If anything, the developments referred to have dealt a foul blow to the Scottsboro defendants." He threatened to quit the case unless the ILD was "removed from the defense."

Following Leibowitz's threat, the defendants and their parents were undecided about who would represent them, the New York attorney or the ILD. On February 15, 1935, however, it was Leibowitz who stood before eight of the highest judges in the country (the ninth, Justice James Clark McReynolds, was absent from the court). The New York lawyer told the justices that Alabama law did not exclude Negroes from the jury rolls, but that "there was a long and unbroken tradition of systematic exclusion . . . throughout the state." Then he presented them with the Jackson County jury rolls which had been forged to prove his point. On April 1, Chief Justice Charles Evans Hughes spoke for the court in *Norris v. Alabama*. "There is no controversy as to the constitutional principle involved," he said. When people are excluded from jury service solely because of their race or color "in the criminal prosecution of a person of the African race, the equal protection of the laws is denied to him, contrary to the Fourteenth Amendment of the Constitution of the United States." As Leibowitz had hoped, the Supreme Court ruled that "the judgment must be reversed and the cause remanded [returned] for further proceedings not inconsistent with this opinion."

Patterson's case presented a dilemma. The US Supreme Court wasn't in the habit of weighing in on decisions made by lower courts that were based on technical issues. But Patterson's case had failed at the state level because of a technical issue, a missed filing deadline. This meant the US Supreme Court justices were faced with ignoring Patterson, and thereby sending him to the electric chair, while granting Norris a new trial. Yet the circumstances of jury selection in each case were identical. In *Patterson v. Alabama*, the justices decided that "the state court should have an opportunity to examine its powers in the light of" the Norris ruling. It set aside the judgment against Patterson and returned the case to the state court for a new trial.

Alabama Governor Bibb Graves almost immediately set about

ordering jury commissioners throughout the state to include Negroes on their rosters of potential jurors. Yet, despite the governor's call to admit the names of blacks to jury lists, there were still politicians who sought "new devices against bona fide admission of the Negro to jury service." In other words, they would look for ways to prevent blacks from being seated on juries. As *New York Times* reporter John Temple Graves wrote, "Many Alabamians . . . will insist that a fresh start be made now in the business of getting the accused men to the electric chair."

At the end of April, Leibowitz wrote to Governor Graves to say he believed it unwise to prosecute the Scottsboro defendants any further, calling the state's star witness a "veteran harlot and jail bird" and the trials thus far "a mockery of justice." He asked the governor to pardon all nine defendants or, if that wasn't possible, to set up an impartial committee to review the facts in the case. He was certain such a committee would find the case lacked merit. "Subversive elements [the ILD and its communist allies]," he wrote, "have exploited the unfortunate plight of these hapless youths for the purpose of raising huge sums of money with which to carry on political propaganda avowedly seeking to tear down our form of government." His letter was answered with silence.

On May 1, 1935, Victoria Price "swore to nine new warrants charging the nine Negro defendants with attacking her." Once the jury rolls had been revised to add the names of blacks, the Scottsboro Boys would face a new set of trials. Clarence Norris reflected, "We had been in jail for over four years, shuttling back and forth between Decatur, Birmingham and Montgomery [Kilby Prison], from cell to cell and trial to trial. I wondered how much longer the state of Alabama would spend its money to prosecute nine innocent boys in order to send them to their deaths. I couldn't understand it then or now, the hatred."

Samuel Leibowitz, second from left, talks defense strategy with seven of the Scottsboro defendants in May 1935. Pictured, from the left, are Deputy Sheriff Charles McComb, Leibowitz, Roy Wright, Olen Montgomery, Ozie Powell, Willie Roberson, Eugene

8

A FAIR TRIAL

Even as Ruby Bates spoke to large crowds "around the country telling of the frame-up," and the mothers of several of the boys, including Patterson, lobbied President Franklin D. Roosevelt to save the young men, a new grand jury was called in Scottsboro. For the first time in sixty years, according to a *New York Times* article, a black man sat on a Jackson County grand jury. Creed Conyers was a farmer and "chairman of the Board of Trustees of Negro Schools" in Paint Rock. Once again, Victoria Price told her tale, and on November 13, 1935, the grand jury issued new, formal indictments against the nine men. "I don't know how the black man voted," Norris wrote later, "but under Alabama law only a two-thirds majority was necessary to return the indictment." Turning his thoughts to Price, he commented, "I have often wondered how she slept nights."

In 1935, after much haggling over the course of the year, the ILD and the NAACP joined with several other organizations to form the Scottsboro Defense Committee (SDC). Among the groups making up the SDC were the American Civil Liberties Union (ACLU), a group dedicated to preserving the Constitution and its guarantees for everyone; the League for Industrial Democracy (LID), which supported the labor union movement; the Methodist Federation for Social Service, which worked for justice among the poor; and the

"HELP US SAVE OUR BOYS"

Several of the boys' mothers spoke at communist party rallies across the United States and abroad to raise money for their sons' defense. In this composite photo are (front row, from left) Josephine Powell, Viola Montgomery, Mamie Williams, and (back row, from left) Ada Wright, Janie Patterson, and Ida Norris.

American Scottsboro Committee (ASC), whose main purpose was to aid in the defense of the boys but which also backed Leibowitz as the boys' primary attorney. The SDC would take over the defense of the nine men. One of the things they quickly realized from the previous trials was that the defense's ties to the ILD and communism added to the prejudice experienced in Alabama. What's more, they came to understand that Leibowitz was a handicap in the Deep South state of Alabama. Alabamians resented him as much as they disapproved of the communists. The SDC decided Leibowitz should take a back seat in the new round of trials, and Clarence Watts, a Huntsville attorney recommended to the defense by Judge Horton, would take the lead role. Watts firmly believed the young men were innocent, but also held to traditional southern thought that blacks as a group were inferior to whites. Even so, the SDC believed the boys had a stronger chance for acquittal with an Alabamian defending them. By taking the case, Watts lost several Huntsville clients.

As Patterson's newest jury was chosen in Judge Callahan's court in Decatur, twelve Negroes were among one hundred prospective jurors in the pool—though they weren't allowed to sit in the jury box where the whites were seated. Patterson observed, "They were afraid, and they got off for one excuse or another. That was okay with me. I didn't want no scared Negroes judging me." Five blacks remained after the others were eliminated, but these five were rejected by the prosecution. Once again, Patterson would be judged by an all-white jury.

Patterson's trial, his fourth, got underway on Tuesday morning, January 21, 1936, before Judge Callahan. As in the previous hearing, the judge hurried things along, shutting down any attempt by Watts to inquire into Price's background once she took the stand as the state's witness. He declared that questions about who accompanied her and Bates to Chattanooga and what the women did when they arrived there were "immaterial." Despite the restrictions, Watts uncovered several contradictions in Price's testimony.

Orville Gilley, who had taken the stand to support Price's story at the previous trial, was now unavailable. A week earlier, in Tennessee, he had been arrested, tried, and convicted of assaulting and robbing two women. Instead, Attorney General Knight called Obie Golden, a guard at Kilby Prison. Golden claimed that Patterson had confessed to the crime one night. Watts objected, but Judge Callahan allowed the guard's testimony into the record. Although Watts led the defense, Leibowitz jumped in to ask the guard if he had reported the confession to the prison warden or to Knight or to any other official, given its importance. Had he written down that night's conversation with Patterson?

He had not.

When Leibowitz tried to use the train model and have a witness identify where he saw Price, the judge refused to allow it. He doubted the model represented the actual train. When R. S. Turner, the conductor on the train, said the model was an exact reproduction, the judge began to ask his own questions of the witness. When Turner held his ground, Judge Callahan ended the examination. "That strikes me as enough of that," he said. "We are magnifying things that are not particularly important."

Within five hours of the trial's start, Watts moved for a mistrial, citing the judge's irritability and impatience. A fair trial was impossible, said Watts, because of Judge Callahan's tendency "to minimize the importance of the evidence offered for the defendant." Looking "sizzling mad," the judge denied the motion and suggested to Watts that he and the defense could take up their complaints in appeals court.

On Wednesday, Melvin C. Hutson summed up the prosecution's case for Knight, urging the jurors to protect the women of Alabama by reaching a guilty verdict. Reminding them that they would have

Protesters march in New York City in support of the Scottsboro Boys. The hooded figure represents Judge W. W. Callahan, who rushed through the trials.

to face their neighbors, he said, "Don't go out and quibble over the evidence. Say to yourselves 'we're tired of this job and put it behind you. Get it done quick and protect the fair womanhood of this great State.'" Watts, on the other hand, quietly asked the jurors to weigh the evidence. "It takes courage to do the right thing," he said, "in the face of public clamor for the wrong thing, but when justice is not administered fairly, governments disintegrate and there is no protection for any one, man or woman, black or white."

In giving his instructions to the jury, Judge Callahan reminded them that the defendant is innocent until proved guilty. That might have been fine had he not also told them that Price was a white woman and "they must assume she did not yield willingly to the Negro defendant." Author Carlton Beals, who covered the case for the *Nation* magazine, believed Callahan's directions left the jury with no choice but to find Patterson guilty.

While Patterson's jury was deliberating his fate on Thursday, the attorneys began selecting a jury for the trial of Clarence Norris, which was scheduled to begin on Friday, January 24. Watts found three in the jury pool who had served on the previous trials of either Patterson or Norris, although they had not informed anyone of this fact. They were promptly dismissed. As the last juror was accepted, the foreman of the Patterson jury sent word that it had reached a verdict. Patterson was certain the finding would be death. Indeed, the jury found him guilty but the jurors "fixed his punishment at seventy-five years in the penitentiary." It was a victory, of a sort; Patterson's life had been spared, but still he was disappointed. "I'd rather die," he said, "than spend another day in jail for something I didn't do."

Price, hearing the verdict, also expressed disappointment. "'Twant fair," she said, again and again.

On Friday, the defense attorneys requested a delay in Norris's trial. They wanted Dr. Bridges to testify, but he had fallen ill. Knight had allowed the doctor's testimony from the first trial to be read into the record in Patterson's trial. Now he blamed this medical evidence for Patterson's sentence of seventy-five years rather than the death penalty he had urged the jury to impose. Knight hoped Judge Callahan's impatience and rush to end the trials would play to his favor, so he stipulated that he would accept nothing less than an actual appearance by the doctor. But, surprising both sides, the judge announced an indefinite recess until Dr. Bridges was well enough to testify.

That afternoon, the defense attorneys left for their homes. Given Patterson's seventy-five-year sentence, they were hopeful for the cases that lay ahead. Their optimism, however, soon faded. As state highway patrol and sheriff's officers drove the defendants in three cars to the Birmingham jail, some eighty miles away, a scuffle broke out. About twenty miles outside of Decatur, Ozie Powell, who rode in the back seat of the middle car and was handcuffed to Norris, whipped out a knife with his free hand and slashed the throat of Deputy Sheriff Edgar Blalock, a passenger in the front seat. Blalock pulled out his weapon to defend himself, and in the struggle that followed, the gun went off, shooting Powell in the head. Blalock was taken to a nearby hospital, where he was treated for a non-life-threatening wound and released. Thomas Knight, the lead prosecutor in the Scottsboro Boys' case and now the lieutenant governor, had been following the convoy in his own vehicle. When he came upon the scene, he refused to let Powell be taken to the hospital with Blalock. Powell didn't receive treatment until after he arrived in Birmingham, where the bullet was removed from his brain. He was given a fifty-fifty chance of recovering, which he did, but with brain damage. As Norris said, "He was never the same as he was, not as bright or intelligent."

In the weeks that followed, two versions of the incident emerged. According to the official report, "the three manacled Negroes were upon the Sheriff and his deputy," in a planned escape attempt. Sheriff

J. Street Sandlin, the driver of the vehicle, said that had he and Blalock not been able to take care of themselves they would have been killed. He claimed that not a word passed from front seat to back, and that Andy Wright, who was seated behind him, was also involved in the attack. Although at first he reported that only Powell was armed, he now said that Wright also had a knife. It was, in the opinion of the report that exonerated the sheriff and his deputy, an unprovoked attack. Norris, who was seated between Powell and Wright, handcuffed to each of them, told a different story. In Norris's recollection, Blalock started off cussing the boys' lawyers, telling the three that they would have "come out a damn sight better if we had Southern lawyers." When Powell became disrespectful, "Blalock wheeled around and slapped him." Then Blalock said, "These sons of bitches should have been killed a long time ago—riding up and down the highway like white people." At that point Powell pulled out the knife, and the struggle began. After getting the careening vehicle under control and braking at the roadside, Sandlin jumped out. Blalock, injured, staggered to the front of the car and collapsed. Seeing his deputy, the sheriff hollered, "I am going to get rid of all these sons of bitches right now!" And he fired. When other officials began to arrive at the scene, Sandlin was prevented from firing at anyone else.

A satisfactory account of the events that afternoon never did become known. Outside the state, the officers' version of the incident was treated with skepticism. Inside Alabama, it created a tension that didn't bode well for the future trials of the Scottsboro Boys. By December 1936, however, the public's tension was replaced by weariness with the entire case.

Knight and the state's new attorney general, A. A. Carmichael, went to New York to meet with Leibowitz. Alabama newspapers whispered that some sort of compromise might be in the works, but the two men denied it. A compromise, however, is exactly what was afoot.

Despite their denial of any deal, Carmichael and Knight met with Leibowitz over the Christmas holidays and proposed to let some of the boys go free—Roy Wright and Eugene Williams, the two youngest, and Olen Montgomery. Willie Roberson likely would have been included in this group because of his age and physical condition, but he wasn't mentioned by name. They would do this in exchange for guilty pleas from Patterson, Norris, and the others. Leibowitz walked away from their offer. His entire argument had been that the young men were innocent. Expecting this, the two Alabama politicians had a backup plan. They wanted the black youths to plead guilty to vagrancy or to fighting with the white boys so the state could save face. Eventually, they reached an agreement. Leibowitz said he would withdraw Patterson's appeal, and the state would charge Ozie Powell only with the assault on Blalock. Charlie Weems, Andy Wright, and Clarence Norris would plead guilty to assault and receive sentences of less than five years. The compromise also allowed for Patterson to be released after serving no more time than Weems, Andy Wright, and Norris.

The SDC at first shot down the compromise when Leibowitz presented it to them. Its members reasoned that pleading guilty to assault of any type would be admitting that the young men were culpable in Price's claims. Leibowitz didn't like the terms either, but he argued that taking them to trial before white southern juries was even riskier. The SDC finally agreed that while it could not endorse the compromise, it would not oppose it. When Carmichael's assistant presented the agreement to Judge Callahan, though, the judge angrily announced that he would have no part of it. He declared that the rape trials would resume in July.

In May 1937, Thomas Knight Jr. died suddenly. Although he

had been unshakable in his prosecution of the Scottsboro Boys, making his political career on their backs, time and their continuing appeals had softened his stance. With his death, the chances for a new compromise brightened even more. Some Alabama newspapers that had trumpeted the death penalty for the young men since 1931 were now writing that nothing could be gained by further prosecution. Even as the Alabama Supreme Court upheld Patterson's conviction on June 14, the state's newspapers were supporting a compromise. Judge Callahan remained the obstacle.

Leibowitz and Clarence Watts had no alternative except to prepare for the July trials of Clarence Norris, Charlie Weems, and the others.

9

HALF OUT AND HALF IN

Clarence Norris went on trial for the third time on July 12, 1937, in a courtroom so steamy that Judge Callahan even had to step down from his high bench to the main floor to escape the worst of the heat. With the death of Knight, Assistant Attorney General Thomas Lawson would handle the prosecution. Attorney General Carmichael had left the state for a vacation retreat. Assisting Lawson was H. G. Bailey, the original Jackson County prosecutor in Scottsboro.

As before, the prosecution began its case with Victoria Price testifying. As Norris recalled, "A child would have known she was lying. She contradicted herself and every other sentence was 'I don't know' or 'I can't recollect.'" The defense took a different tack this time. Leibowitz read into the record the original testimony of Dr. R. R. Bridges, who had died in March 1936, shortly after Patterson's trial. Then Watts called two witnesses to discredit Price's testimony. They were Richard S. Watson and Sol Wallace, police officers from Price's hometown of Huntsville. Wallace had known Price since 1921, and Watson, since 1924. Both officers admitted "her reputation generally was bad" and Watson said, "I would not believe her under oath." The verdict was as Leibowitz feared. Medical evidence suggesting no rape had taken place and the statements by the two Huntsville officers did not enter into the all-white jury's decision process.

New Trials in Decatur

William Washington Callahan,

presiding judge

FOR THE PROSECUTION:

Thomas S. Lawson, assistant attorney general of
Alabama; **H. G. Bailey**, Jackson County circuit
solicitor; **Melvin C. Hutson**, Morgan County solicitor

FOR THE DEFENSE:

Clarence Watts, Huntsville attorney (lead);
Samuel S. Leibowitz, New York attorney (assisting)

STAR WITNESS FOR THE PROSECUTION:

Victoria Price

WHO WAS ON TRIAL (SEPARATELY):

Clarence Norris, **Andy Wright**, **Charlie Weems**,
Ozie Powell

WITNESSES FOR THE DEFENSE:

Richard S. Watson, Huntsville police officer;
Sol Wallace, Huntsville police officer

After only two and a half hours of deliberation, Norris was found guilty and sentenced to death.

Callahan wanted to begin the trials of the other defendants right away, but Watts asked for a delay. At first, Callahan was reluctant, but when Watts rose before the judge, he swayed and then collapsed. The judge put off the remaining trials until a later date.

Callahan wasn't the only one impatient to have the trials end. Melvin C. Hutson, the Morgan County solicitor helping to prosecute the case, was eager to speed things along also. On July 18, the prosecutor told news reporters, "Two of the Negroes whom we regard as the ringleaders of the crime have been convicted. One of them, Clarence Norris, has been condemned to die in the electric chair. The other, Heywood [sic] Patterson, has been sentenced to imprisonment for seventy-five years. We are satisfied that a third Negro [Ozie Powell], who took a leading part in the crime, is not fit mentally or physically to stand trial." When asked how he planned to speed through the remaining trials of Charlie Weems, Andy Wright, Willie Roberson, Olen Montgomery, and the two youngest defendants, Roy Wright and Eugene Williams, he wasn't specific. He said only, "One never can tell what may happen."

At the outset of Andy Wright's trial on July 19, the prosecution announced that it would seek a life sentence rather than the death penalty. In exchange, Leibowitz, with Watts still unable to resume his defense, agreed to select twelve jurymen from a smaller pool of potential jurors. "It seems to me," he said, "that one [group of] twelve is about as good as another." Meanwhile, even the state's prosecutors must have begun to doubt Price's story, if indeed they had ever truly believed it. They met privately with the accuser to say she could retract her charge without fear of prosecution for perjury. She refused.

Wright's trial went like the others, starting with Price telling

In this July 12, 1937, photo, some of the men play music in the Birmingham jail as they await their hearings before Judge William Washington Callahan in Decatur. Pictured are (from the left) Olen Montgomery, Andy Wright, Eugene Williams, Charlie Weems, Haywood Patterson, Clarence Norris (dancing), Roy Wright, Ozie Powell, and Willie Roberson.

her oft-repeated story. When Bailey closed for the state, he attacked New York rather than the merits of the defense's case. Responding to this, a frustrated Leibowitz told the jury, "I can't fight that kind of thing. I'm entitled to an acquittal in this case." Bailey's attacks on New York, he said, were the prosecution's "knockout punch." Leibowitz believed there was sufficient doubt in the truthfulness of Price's story to clear Wright, indeed to have cleared all the young men. But the jury condemned him to ninety-nine years' imprisonment. When Callahan passed judgment, he asked Wright if he had anything to say. Shuffling his feet and looking at the floor, Wright said, "I ain't got justice here."

When the Weems trial began on Thursday, July 22, Leibowitz seethed with anger that he hadn't been able to surmount the jurors' prejudice and hate at the Wright proceedings. When Price took the witness chair, he attacked her like a swarm of inflamed wasps. He shouted his questions at her, and she just as quickly bellowed defiant answers, until she became so confused she began contradicting herself. Callahan stepped in to warn Leibowitz: "It is not too late," he cautioned, "for the court to enforce its orders. Your manner is going to lead to trouble." Lunch recess is probably all that saved Leibowitz from a contempt-of-court charge.

That afternoon, the defense attorney asked the judge to remove the jury so he could make a motion. With the jury gone, Leibowitz said, "I move that the testimony of Victoria Price be stricken from the record on the ground that her testimony is so rampant with perjury that the court is constrained—" Callahan, his face flushed with anger, cut him off to deny the motion.

The next day, as Leibowitz wrapped up the Weems trial, he was unrestrained and spoke at length to the jury, as well as to the reporters in the courtroom. As with Andy Wright, the state had not sought the death penalty. But it was as if the floodgates of frustration opened and poured forth. An attorney's closing argument is the one time during the course of a trial that the judge is forbidden to interrupt and opposing counsel may not object. Leibowitz accused the farmers who testified for the state of being "trained seals" and "performers in a flea circus." He said the notion of a black man being able to receive a fair trial in Alabama was "poppycock." Unable to stop the tirade, Judge Callahan paced back and forth behind the bench. Thomas Lawson left the courtroom entirely. And still Leibowitz protested, shouting, "I'm sick and tired of this sanctimonious hypocrisy. It isn't Charlie Weems on trial in this case. It's a Jew lawyer and New York State put on trial here by the inflammatory remarks of Mr. Bailey."

The jury deliberated for two hours and twenty-five minutes. It returned a guilty verdict and set the punishment at seventy-five years in the state penitentiary.

As soon as Judge Callahan informed Weems of the jury's decision, Ozie Powell was led into the courtroom by Sheriff Sandlin. Lawson had agreed that he would drop the rape indictment against Powell and charge him only with the assault on Deputy Blalock. Leibowitz explained to his client what was happening, and then brought him to the bench. The judge asked him if he was guilty or not guilty. Powell replied, "I'm guilty of cutting the deputy." The judge sentenced him to the maximum possible—twenty years.

It was almost noon on Saturday, July 24, when Thomas Lawson walked to the bench. In a whispered conversation with the judge, he dropped all charges against the remaining defendants—Eugene Williams, Roy Wright, Olen Montgomery, and Willie Roberson. They were free to go. Leibowitz immediately dashed across the lawn to the jail, handed the court order to one of the deputies, and then, with his four clients, ducked into two waiting cars. "Neither the Sheriff nor the prisoners had been told in advance of the State's plan."

Charlie Weems and Clarence Norris read a newspaper after Norris's third conviction. At the 1937 trial, Norris was sentenced to death in Alabama's electric chair, nicknamed Yellow Mama after being painted with highway department road-striping paint.

The boys thought they were being taken back to the Birmingham jail and trooped outside like well-trained prisoners, "with their hands above their heads." Their departure, with a police escort to the state line, was swift and was made public only after they were out of town. Leibowitz waited until they were safely away before telling his clients that they were free. Hearing this news, Montgomery said, "Gee, I haven't been so happy since I was 2 years old." Not everyone was as jubilant. "It was the saddest day of my life," Norris recalled, years later, about learning the news. Patterson agreed with Norris: "For the boys *let off* it was a victory. For those of us *dealt off* it was something else."

To explain why they had withdrawn charges against the remaining defendants, the prosecutors released a statement that raised as many questions as it settled. While maintaining the guilt of the young men who had been tried and convicted, they pointed to medical evidence to conclude that neither Willie Roberson nor Olen Montgomery could possibly have participated in the fight with the white boys or an attack on the women. The former was so sick with venereal disease he could barely move; the latter could hardly see. This, the statement explained, was "a case of mistaken identity." As to the two who were juveniles at the time of the alleged crime, the state reasoned that after six and a half years in jail, justice had been served.

Editorials in newspapers questioned the prosecutors' statement, asking why four men were sentenced to either prison or death if Price's identification of even some of them was mistaken. Couldn't she have been mistaken about all of them? How could some of the men and boys be innocent but the others guilty on the same evidence? As Norris wrote later, "If five of us were innocent of rape, four of us couldn't be guilty." The editors wondered why Roberson and Montgomery, who were clearly innocent based on the prosecution's own statement, were not compensated for their years lost behind bars. In the past, others who had been falsely accused and incarcerated had received compensation. Norris asked, "Weren't we either all guilty or all innocent?" Indeed, newspapers across the country—from the *New York Times* to the *Montgomery* [Alabama] *Advertiser*—looked at the prosecution's statement and determined that "either all were guilty or none was guilty."

Leibowitz agreed. He told the press, "It is nothing short of a miracle that the boys were saved from the chair, and it's God's wonder that they are actually free. I can hardly believe it. We'll keep up the fight until all of these innocent boys are saved." Despite the lawyer's vow, the young men who had been tried and convicted and now sat behind bars felt abandoned, betrayed by American justice and even by their New York attorney.

Delivering another blow to the condemned men, on October 26, 1937, the United States Supreme Court declined to review Patterson's conviction. "I knew I was going to be kept in prison," he later wrote. The defense knew that the state's case against the other imprisoned men was equally strong, but Allan Knight Chalmers, chairman of the Scottsboro Defense Committee, wasn't ready to give up hope. He decided to appeal to Governor Bibb Graves.

Chalmers sent Graves a letter on November 11, 1937. He asked for a meeting with the governor to discuss the Scottsboro case. He pointed out that Alabama was in a vulnerable position, having released some of the defendants. Surprisingly, Graves agreed to a conference.

At the meeting, Chalmers warned the governor that as long as Patterson, Norris, Wright, and Weems remained in prison, the national press would continue to criticize Alabama. Grover Cleveland Hall, a newspaperman and editor of the *Montgomery Advertiser*, was also at the meeting and supported pardons for the four men. He promised Graves full support in his newspaper and said the Birmingham newspapers were with him if the governor chose to release the men.

Olen Montgomery, wearing glasses (third from left), and Eugene Williams, wearing suspenders (fourth from left), arriving at Pennsylvania Station in New York in 1937 after the assault charges against them were dropped. The charges against Willie Roberson and Roy Wright were dropped at the same time. They also traveled to New York with Montgomery and Williams and their attorney Samuel Leibowitz.

Samuel Leibowitz, center, stands in his New York office with the four freed Scottsboro Boys (from the left): Willie Roberson, Eugene Williams, Roy Wright, and Olen Montgomery.

Governor Graves listened intently to Chalmers and Hall, and then said, "I cannot make any promise which would look like a deal. I have already stated my feeling that the position of the State is untenable [indefensible] with half out and half in on the same charges and evidence."

Throughout the spring of 1938, Governor Graves begged for patience as he weighed his decision. Then, in midsummer, the Alabama Supreme Court delivered another blow to the defense. It upheld Norris's death sentence, which was set for August 19. A week earlier, the "court affirmed . . . long-term sentences for Andy Wright and Charlie Weems." All hope seemed lost.

But on July 5, there appeared to be a glimmer of optimism. Governor Graves commuted Norris's death sentence to life imprisonment. Norris's life would be spared. Not long after, word came down to Chalmers that Graves was ready to respond to the requests for pardons for the five imprisoned men.

As Norris recalled, "Dr. Chalmers was assured by the governor that all of us except Ozie Powell would be released October 31, 1938. We were to be on parole for six months, then we'd be on our own. Our relatives prepared places for us to live, either with them or nearby. The SDC would act as our guardian and provide the opportunity for us to go to school, learn a trade and otherwise be rehabilitated."

On October 29, Governor Graves interviewed the men. Chalmers already had made elaborate plans for their release, but that same night Graves sent an urgent telegram to Chalmers: "Please defer Mondays engagement until further notice. Am not ready to act. Please acknowledge receipt." On November 15, his decision was announced: "Governor Graves denied today pardon applications of 5 'Scottsboro rape case' convicts." Norris picked up the story, writing that the governor "refused to pardon us because [he said] we were all sassy to him" when he interviewed them. He continued, "He reneged on his promise to Dr. Chalmers and he lied to the public. There was too much at stake not to be on our best behavior when we saw the governor. He had our freedom in his hands and we wanted it."

In an attempt to get the governor to live up to his agreement, Chalmers made public their correspondence. But Governor Graves remained firm. Wright, Weems, Powell, and Norris "settled into the penitentiary life at Kilby." Patterson, said to be a troublemaker by the Kilby warden, was transferred to Atmore Prison Farm, about which Patterson wrote, "The people all over the state of Alabama, they call that place *Murderers' Home.*"

OBSCURITY

10

As the Scottsboro case faded from the headlines at the end of the 1930s, the SDC began to lose the donors it relied on for funding. People were now preoccupied with the rise of Adolf Hitler in Germany and the outbreak of World War II. Allan Knight Chalmers continued to fight for pardons for all the imprisoned defendants through a campaign of letter writing, but he no longer had the strength of a healthy organization behind him. The four released Scottsboro defendants didn't help his cause. Leibowitz had originally planned for the boys to receive job training, but they were lured away by vaudeville and the quick money it promised. When they became disillusioned with show business and decided to leave, they had no training for anything else. They were nearly illiterate, and prison had not prepared them to hold jobs.

After his brief stint on the vaudeville circuit, Olen Montgomery joined Roy Wright on a two-and-a-half month, nationwide speaking tour to help raise money for the SDC. The NAACP paid for Montgomery to receive music lessons, because he said he wanted to be a musician, but he soon turned to drink. He often refused work, usually saying he was too ill. He spent the rest of his life moving around the country—Atlanta, Georgia; Detroit, Michigan; New York; and Hartford, Connecticut—and getting in scrapes with

140

the law. Whenever he decided on a change of scenery, he turned to the NAACP for handouts and financial help. If support wasn't forthcoming, he'd threaten to make trouble that would embarrass the group. The organization's leaders almost always gave in to his demands. In 1940, Roy Wilkins, with the NAACP, wrote about him, saying, "The damage which was done to Olen by his imprisonment in Alabama is a great tragedy and one which has already had an effect upon his whole life." Montgomery eventually returned to Monroe, Georgia, the town where he had been born. The date of his death is unknown.

Leroy "Roy" Wright was probably the most successful of the four, at least for a time. Unhappy with the money he was earning, he quickly grew disappointed with vaudeville and broke with the manager who had coaxed the four youths away from Leibowitz and the SDC. After he and Montgomery completed their speaking tour for the SDC, Wright got help from Bill "Bojangles" Robinson, a popular entertainer. Robinson offered to pay for Wright to attend vocational school. Wright later served in the army and joined the merchant marines. In 1959, after a long time at sea, he returned to find his wife with another man. Believing she had been unfaithful, he shot her, in a fit of rage, and then turned the gun on himself, committing suicide.

Little is known about what became of Eugene Williams. In New York, he told Leibowitz he wanted to join a jazz orchestra, but after a while he told the lawyer he wanted to go to Saint Louis, Missouri, where he had relatives to help him. Chalmers hoped that when Williams got there he would enroll in a Baptist seminary. Williams settled into life in the city, but whether he ever fulfilled Chalmers's wishes for him isn't clear. There is no information about his death.

Willie Roberson had made it through seventh grade in Atlanta, but doctors in prison calculated his IQ at around sixty-four and

The four freed Scottsboro Boys, with their lawyer Samuel Leibowitz, attend a rally to welcome the young men to New York.

Roy Wright with his mother, Ada, on July 31, 1937, after Alabama dropped the charges against him and he was released from prison.

his mental age at nine. Throughout his time in prison he suffered from asthma, which was worsened by the cold, damp air in the windowless cells. Some nights, he said, he was unable to breathe. He wasn't treated for his venereal disease until 1933. After the Alabama courts dropped the charges against him, Roberson lived in New York City, where he worked steadily in menial jobs. He died of a severe asthma attack, but the date of his death is unknown.

In Alabama, the legislature set up a new, three-member Pardons and Paroles Board in 1939. In February of 1940, it met to consider parole requests Chalmers filed for Clarence Norris, Andy Wright, Charlie Weems, Haywood Patterson, and Ozie Powell. The men claimed to have "suffered sufficiently." The *Corpus Christi Caller-Times*, of Corpus Christi, Texas, called it "the most ticklish problem it [the board] probably will ever face—the notorious Scottsboro case." The board, on March 8, turned down the parole requests but promised that "a day for reconsideration in each case will be set in accordance with our judgment."

Finally, in November 1943, the Alabama Pardons and Paroles Board quietly released Charlie Weems. He had been serving a seventy-five-year sentence, and now was in his early thirties. While in prison, according to Norris, "A guard attacked him [Weems] with a baling hook, ripped Charlie's chest open and cut his throat. He was hospitalized for months in a serious condition." The attack was a case of mistaken identity. The guard was temporarily suspended, but later reinstated. Weems was released to the jurisdiction of the Georgia State Parole Board to work in a laundry. He married, but little is known about his life after that. There are no details about his death.

In January 1944, the board paroled Andy Wright and Clarence Norris. The NAACP had obtained jobs for the men at a smelting plant in Cleveland, Ohio, for forty dollars per week. Despite this opportunity, they were sent to work at a lumberyard near Alabama's

Clarence Norris walks through a cell gate at Kilby Prison in 1946 after having been granted a second parole.

state capital. Describing their new environment on the "free streets," Norris wrote: "It might as well have been a prison camp. The place was owned by a man named Easley. He had built all these little houses and most of his employees lived on the premises. So we paid our salaries back to him in rent. The pay was thirty-five cents an hour. The rent was seven dollars a week." Continuing, he said, "Andy and me shared a room, eight by ten feet, and we had to sleep in the same bed, with one pillow. We were assigned the hardest work. The foreman cussed us all the time. . . . They wanted us to do something that would get them stirred up enough to lynch us." The pair soon broke parole and fled to New York, but Chalmers and the NAACP talked them into returning to Alabama. Despite promises to Chalmers from the Pardons and Paroles Board that the men would be given another chance, they were returned to Kilby Prison. Norris lamented, "I had been free for nine months."

In 1946, Ozie Powell was paroled, and Norris was given a second chance at freedom. Powell went to Georgia, where he evidently settled into a life of obscurity. Nothing is known about him after prison. Norris, on the other hand, had no intention of reporting to the Alabama job the Pardons and Paroles Board had arranged for him. He caught a train to Atlanta and from there went to Cleveland, where his mother lived. He assumed his brother's name, found a job, and got married. When agents from the Federal Bureau of Investigation (FBI) came to his mother's place looking for him, he said, "My name is Willie Norris." He showed them his false identification papers, and they left. In 1953, after his marriage didn't work out, Norris moved to New York City and eventually worked for the city.

From Atmore, Haywood Patterson had been transferred back to Kilby Prison. Allan Knight Chalmers visited him there and said, "They tell me your prison record is not good." In front of the warden, Patterson fired back, "No damn record keeping me here,

Dr. Chalmers. I am kept here by the same thing that brought me here, prejudice and hate." Eventually, he lost hope of ever receiving a pardon, and fell into a prison routine. But he was making plans and waiting for warm weather, when the convicts would return to work in the prison's fields. Patterson told a fellow prisoner who worked in the laundry, "I am giving myself a pardon any day now." The laundry worker set aside some civilian clothes for him.

Then one hot July day in 1948, Patterson put on his prison clothes over the civilian ones the laundry worker had saved for him. It was time to put his plan into action. He and the other convicts went to work in the fields that day as usual, but on their way back to Kilby, he and eight others attempted their escapes. Patterson fled into the corn fields. "Prison Director Frank Boswell said Patterson was the first to leap from a truck as it rounded a curve. A guard fired once with a shotgun and then emptied his revolver at the convicts as they ran through a corn field but failed to halt them." Patterson later wrote, "I began to change clothes right there, right down in the corn. Stripped right down to my civilian clothes." He eluded prison guards, who searched with dogs, and a hunt by airplanes for a week. He didn't stop running until he reached his sister's house in Detroit.

During his years in prison, Patterson had taught himself to read and write by using a dictionary and a Bible. While in Detroit, he worked with journalist Earl Conrad to write his autobiography, which was published in 1950. Patterson was eventually caught by the FBI, but the governor of Michigan refused to send him back to Alabama. In December of that year, he was involved in a bar fight that resulted in a stabbing death. After several trials, he was convicted of manslaughter and sentenced to between six and sixteen years in prison. He served only one year, dying of cancer in jail on August 24, 1952.

In June 1950, nineteen years after being rounded up from the train in Paint Rock, the last of the Scottsboro Boys still in prison was ordered released. Andy Wright, then thirty-eight years old, was given his second parole after he told the board, "I believe I can make a go of it." Chalmers had arranged a job for him as an orderly at a hospital in Albany, New York. As he walked out of Kilby Prison a free man, Wright told reporters, "I've got no hard feelings toward anyone." A little over a year after his release from prison, he stood once again accused of rape. A woman he was dating said he had raped her thirteen-year-old daughter. Wright was acquitted of the charge by an all-white jury, when defense attorneys provided by the NAACP proved the woman had a personal grudge against him and had lied. In subsequent years, Wright encountered more bad luck. He married but found little work, and he stabbed his wife during an argument. Although she refused to press charges, he felt the need to leave New York. He settled in Connecticut. There he fell into obscurity.

Fame often is fleeting, and so it was for Victoria Price and Ruby Bates. Price was bitter that the nine men were freed and that the state abandoned her. The mill she worked in closed, and she left Alabama for Tennessee. Chalmers heard that she was willing to renounce her accusations and testimony, so he sent an investigator from the SDC to meet with her. She agreed to take it all back—for a hefty price. Chalmers refused to have anything to do with it.

After Bates reversed her testimony, she toured the country briefly as an ILD speaker, but interest in her, the communists, and the case soon faded. While the Alabama prosecutors in the case had insisted Bates was living a life of luxury in a New York City penthouse as payment for recanting her accusation, the reality was that she worked in a factory in upstate New York until she was diagnosed with tuberculosis. She then returned to the South. It was assumed that both Price and Bates died sometime in the early 1960s, but that was not the case.

BACK IN THE HEADLINES

n April 1976, the National Broadcasting Company (NBC) aired a television docudrama called *Judge Horton and the Scottsboro Boys*. Ruby Bates, who was living in Yakima, Washington, surfaced in May to file a $2.5 million libel suit against the network for invading her privacy. A newspaper report revealed that Bates "left her home in Alabama in 1940 to find work, a husband and privacy in Washington state." She married Elmer Schut in 1943, and the couple worked as farm laborers in the Yakima valley. Neither she nor her husband watched the made-for-television program, but she was upset that it had dredged up the case and her role in it again. "I wish the whole thing had never happened," she said. She also was angry that the program said she had died in 1961. "I think it would have been easy for them to find me—if they'd have asked the folks I got scattered all over northern Alabama," she said. Ruby Bates Schut died on October 27, 1976, before the lawsuit was settled.

Price, now Victoria Price Street, also lodged a lawsuit against NBC. She sought $6 million in damages, claiming that the network libeled her "by suggesting she lied during the rape trials." She watched the program and saw herself portrayed as a person of low moral character, a bum, and worse. "I could have sunk through the floor when I seen it," she said. After the Alabama trials and seeking some relief from the notoriety she'd gained, Price moved with her mother from Huntsville to Tennessee, where she married twice. The first marriage was brief, lasting only two days, but then she married a sharecropper named Dean Street. When the lawsuit reached the courtroom of Judge Charles Neese, he dismissed the case after four days of testimony, saying, "There is no evidence of any fault against NBC." Later, on appeal, a settlement was reached out of court. Victoria Price Street died on Sunday, October 17, 1982. She never recanted her story of rape.

Two days before Bates died, Clarence Norris had received favorable news from the Alabama Pardons and Paroles Board. Since 1946, when he broke the conditions of his parole, he had been living as a fugitive. But since fleeing Alabama for the second time, he had married, raised two daughters, and worked steadily as a warehouseman for New York City. "I was tired of being a fugitive," he said. With the help of the NAACP, Norris petitioned Alabama from New York for a pardon. He explained, "Fifteen years is more than long enough to suffer in prison for something I didn't do and then to suffer all these years thinking I might be arrested as a fugitive." He had the support of Alabama's then attorney general, William J. Baxley, who went to bat for Norris. After reviewing the facts of the case, Baxley wrote to the Pardons and Paroles Board and asked that Norris be pardoned. In his letter, the attorney general noted, "In my opinion . . . this individual never should have been charged with any offense against Ruby Bates or Victoria Price, and . . . his repeated sentences of death and his 15 years spent incarcerated in Alabama prisons can only be termed tragic." On October 25, Alabama governor George C. Wallace signed the pardon order for the last known survivor of the Scottsboro trials. In effect, the pardon acknowledged that Norris had never committed the crime of which he'd been accused. Nathaniel Jones, of the NAACP, commented, "While no act

State Board of Pardons and Paroles

Montgomery, Alabama

CERTIFICATE OF PARDON WITH RESTORATION
OF CIVIL AND POLITICAL RIGHTS

KNOW ALL MEN BY THESE PRESENTS:

It having been made to appear to the Alabama State Board of Pardons and Paroles that

_____ Clarence Norris _____ CM ____ #39745 _____

was convicted in____ Morgan _____ County on_____ July 5 ____, 19 38

of_____ Rape _____, was sentenced to a term of____ Life _____ XXXXX

and was released on parole on_____ September 26 ____, 19 46, and the maximum

term of sentence has not yet expired,

NOW, In compliance with the authority vested in the State Board of Pardons and Paroles by the Constitution and the Laws of the State of Alabama to grant pardons and to restore civil and political rights, it is

ORDERED that a pardon be granted to the above named as a result of the above stated conviction, and all prior disqualifying convictions, and it is further ordered that all civil and political rights which were lost as a result of the conviction be and they are hereby restored.

GIVEN UNDER THE HAND AND SEAL of the State Board of Pardons and Paroles,

this the___ 29th day of_____ November _____, 19 76

STATE BOARD OF PARDONS AND PAROLES

By _Norman. F. Ussery_
Chairman

of Alabama can restore to Mr. Norris that of which he was robbed, nor expunge from his memory the long nightmare to which he was subjected, this act of compassion by Governor Wallace and the Alabama Board of Pardons and Paroles is nevertheless praiseworthy." Norris later teamed up with writer Sybil D. Washington to pen a book about his life and the tragedy of the Scottsboro case. Called *The Last of the Scottsboro Boys: An Autobiography*, the book was published in 1979. Norris died in 1989 at the age of seventy-six.

• • •

Justice sometimes boards the wrong train or heads down the wrong track. In the case of the Scottsboro Boys, justice was delayed for decades. But in the mid-1970s, a Scottsboro teen named Shelia Washington stumbled upon a package wrapped in layers of plastic, tucked inside a pillowcase, hidden away under her parents' bed like a long-buried secret. She unwrapped it, and out tumbled "an old, thin paperback," Haywood Patterson's memoir. Washington began to read the account of nine black youths who had been accused of rape by two white women, many of the young men sentenced to years in Alabama's Kilby Prison. One day, as the seventeen-year-old sat on her family's sofa reading about one of America's most infamous miscarriages of justice, her father caught her with the book. Fearful and angered, he hastily grabbed it out of her hands. "You don't need to know about that," he said. "Just keep quiet about this now." Despite her father's warnings, keeping quiet wasn't in Washington's nature. In 1978, her brother was killed by guards in Kilby Prison, where he had been sent after killing a white man in a fight. The story of the nine youths struck a chord with the young woman, who never forgot her father's fear and anger or her brother's death at the hands of prison guards. In 2009, she began a campaign to seek justice for the nine. Washington went before Alabama's Pardons and Paroles Board, only to learn there was no mechanism for granting posthumous pardons.

She turned to Arthur Orr, an Alabama state senator. He recalled the NBC docudrama and was moved by her appeal. He drew up and introduced legislation to allow for posthumous pardons in cases of racial discrimination. Washington wanted not only pardons for the nine but also exonerations, so Orr added a resolution to exonerate the nine men. While pardons excuse the crime and erase the sentences, exonerations go even further. An accused person exonerated of a crime has been declared innocent. By a unanimous vote, the law passed.

In 2013, state senator Arthur Orr introduced a resolution that would exonerate the Scottsboro Boys. It passed the Alabama legislature in a unanimous (twenty-nine to zero) vote. Shelia Washington is seen in the background looking on.

Governor Robert Bentley officially signed the bill and resolution on April 11, 2013. Later, on April 19, a ceremonial signing took place at the Scottsboro Boys Museum and Cultural Center, which Washington had established to help bring the case out of the shadows. Sometimes the justice train is slow arriving, but, as Bentley said, "We need to right the wrongs that have been done in the past. We should never ignore history. It is important to confront our history and secure justice whenever we can." It was too late, of course, for the Scottsboro Boys to bask in their

On April 19, 2013, decades after the Scottsboro trials began, Alabama governor Robert Bentley, seated at center, hands a pen to Clarence Norris Jr., son of Clarence Norris, at a ceremonial signing in Scottsboro. Standing, in white, is Shelia Washington.

exoneration. But Senator Orr described it as a release, a letting go of the past. He said, "Today is a reminder that it is never too late to right a wrong. We cannot go back in time and change the course of history, but we can change how we respond to history. The passage of time and doing nothing is no excuse." The hearing for the legislation he proposed marked "a significant milestone for these young men, their families and for our great state by officially recognizing and correcting a tremendous wrong."

Justice was a long time coming but better late than not at all. It took eighty-two years to right the wrong, a little over eight decades for the Scottsboro Boys to receive their measure of justice. True, it didn't reach them during their lifetimes, but the actions of Governor Bentley, Senator Orr, Shelia Washington, and others tell us we are not the people we were once. Perhaps Governor Bentley said it best: "We cannot take back what happened, but we can make it right by moving forward."

AUTHOR'S NOTE

What happened to the nine youths who became known as the Scottsboro Boys was America at its worst—prejudice, racism, and injustice. We can only speculate how their lives might have taken a different turn if their journey to Memphis had not been interrupted. The emotional and physical scars inflicted on them in prison left the men damaged, some might say beyond repair. They were robbed, not just of their freedom but of their youth and spirit. Changing the past isn't possible, but confronting it and exposing it helps to remind us that we must be vigilant so it won't happen again.

Despite the tragedy of the Scottsboro trials, some good came from them. The 1932 US Supreme Court decision in *Powell v. Alabama* held that the right to adequate, competent legal representation, at least in capital cases, and sufficient time to prepare a defense are among the underlying principles of the due process clause of the Fourteenth Amendment to the US Constitution. The 1935 US Supreme Court decision in *Norris v. Alabama* ruled that the intentional exclusion of African Americans from jury pools is unlawful. These landmark rulings are the legacy the Scottsboro Boys left for future generations.

It is interesting to note that when I visited Scottsboro as part of my research, I was asked by more than a few local persons to explain that if only the youths had traveled a little farther to the west before they were taken into custody, they might have been called the Huntsville Boys. This is true, but it is also a fact that they were apprehended in Jackson County, of which Scottsboro is the seat of government. There is still great embarrassment and resentment among some local people that newspapers of the day tagged the boys with the name of Scottsboro. Some individuals continue to blame the ignorance of the mountain folk who swarmed into the town from the surrounding hills for tarnishing the town's image and for creating the mob-like atmosphere for which Scottsboro became known around the world. To play such "if only" games is to deny Scottsboro's history. The rushed trials, the angry mobs, the injustice happened there—even if it is no longer the town it was. The people I met in Scottsboro were hospitable, warm, and helpful. It is a beautiful area located in the rolling hills of northern Alabama. The historic courthouse with its cupola, the town square around it, and the plaques commemorating the Scottsboro Boys tell me the town has begun to embrace its role in history as a reminder of where we were and of how far we've come in the fight against racial bias and injustice.

When young people read this book, it is my hope that they realize how dangerous lies—even little white lies—can be. Lies have consequences, and sometimes they can be devastating to the people swept up in them.

A note about the young men: Some of them were uncertain about their dates of birth, and records of the time were poorly kept or nonexistent. Roy Wright, for example, was reported in some sources to be twelve and in others to be thirteen. I used his most commonly cited age (thirteen) within the text of the book. Eugene Williams was thought by officials to be older than he was, and his age was variously given. Most sources, however, listed his age at thirteen. Depending on the source, Ozie Powell's age was either sixteen or seventeen, while Charlie Weems age was given as either nineteen or twenty.

Unable to track down birth certificates or death records, I erred on the side of majority opinion. What we are fairly certain of is that Weems was the oldest of the nine and Roy Wright, the youngest.

Victoria Price's age also was at times reported to be twenty-one and at other times, twenty-three or twenty-seven. What we can be sure of is that she was older than Ruby Bates and twice-married, twice-divorced by 1931.

Respectfully, I referred to African Americans in the text as "colored," "black," or "Negro" to help place the story in its proper time. These were the terms used by the nine youths themselves and in the press of the day.

BIBLIOGRAPHY

SOURCES CONSULTED BY THE AUTHOR

Carter, Dan T. *Scottsboro: A Tragedy of the American South*. Baton Rouge: Louisiana State University Press, 1969.

Goodman, James. *Stories of Scottsboro*. New York: Vintage Books, 1995. Originally published by Pantheon Books, 1994.

Haskins, James. *The Scottsboro Boys*. New York: Henry Holt and Company, 1994.

Hughes, Langston. *I Wonder as I Wander*. New York: Hill and Wang, 1993. Originally published by Rinehart, 1956. (primary source)

Kinshasa, Kwando M., ed. *The Scottsboro Boys in Their Own Words: Selected Letters, 1931–1950*. Jefferson, NC: McFarland, 2014. (primary source)

Klanwatch Project of the Southern Poverty Law Center. *Ku Klux Klan: A History of Racism and Violence*. 6th ed. Montgomery, AL: Southern Poverty Law Center, 2011.

Leibowitz, Robert. *The Defender: The Life and Career of Samuel S. Leibowitz, 1893–1933*. Englewood Cliffs, NJ: Prentice-Hall, 1981.

Norris, Clarence, and Sybil D. Washington. *The Last of the Scottsboro Boys: An Autobiography*. New York: G. P. Putnam's Sons, 1979. (primary source)

Patterson, Haywood, and Earl Conrad. *Scottsboro Boy*. Garden City, NY: Doubleday, 1950. (primary source)

Sorensen, Lita. *The Scottsboro Boys Trial: A Primary Source Account*. New York: Rosen Publishing Group, 2004.

U.S. Supreme Court: Records and Briefs, 1832–1978. Print edition. Making of Modern Law series. (primary source)

Newspapers were also consulted to verify accounts in the print sources above and to collect primary-source quotes. These included the *New York Times*, especially articles by F. Raymond Daniell, who was sent to Alabama to cover the trials; the *St. Louis Star and Times* (Saint Louis, MO); the *Pittsburgh Courier* (Pittsburgh, PA); the *Chicago Tribune* (Chicago, IL); the *Anniston Star* (Anniston, AL); the *Manchester Guardian* (Manchester, England), now the *Guardian* (London, England); the *Baltimore Sun* (Baltimore, MD); the *Press-Forum Weekly* (Mobile, AL); the *Morning Call* (Allentown, PA); the *Enterprise-Journal* (McComb, MS); the *Corpus Christi Caller-Times* (Corpus Christi, TX); the *Tucson Daily Citizen* (Tucson, AZ); the *Palladium-Item* (Richmond, IN); the *Montgomery Advertiser* (Montgomery, AL); the *Atlanta Constitution* (Atlanta, GA); the *Jackson County Sentinel* (Scottsboro, AL); the *Progressive Age* (Scottsboro, AL), and others. (primary sources)

INTERVIEW

Shelia Washington, interview by the author, November 18, 2017, Scottsboro Boys Museum and Cultural Center, Scottsboro, AL. (primary source)

FILM/VIDEO

Scottsboro: An American Tragedy. A Social Media Productions, Inc., Production; produced by Daniel Anker and Barak Goodman; written by Barak Goodman for *American Experience*. WGBH Educational Foundation, 2001. DVD.

ON STAGE

The Scottsboro Boys. Music and lyrics by John Kander and Fred Ebb. Book by David Thompson. Originally staged at the Vineyard Theatre, New York, 2010.

WEBSITES AND ONLINE ARTICLES

ACLU History: Scottsboro Boys. aclu.org/other/aclu-history-scottsboro-boys.

Alabama Department of Archives and History. archives.alabama.gov/
searchcoll.html.

"Ala. Parole Board Approves Pardons in 1931 'Scottsboro Boys' Rape
Case." NBC 5 Chicago online, Nov. 21, 2013. nbcchicago.com/news/
national-international/Alabama-Parole-Board-posthumous-pardons-
Scottsboro-Boys-rape-case-232834071.html.

Kelley, Robin D. G. "The Case of the 'Scottsboro Boys'" (unpublished
manuscript, n.d.). writing.upenn.edu/~afilreis/88/scottsboro.html.

Linder, Douglas O. "The Scottsboro Boys." *Famous Trials*. University
of Missouri–Kansas City Law School. famous-trials.com/
scottsboroboys/1562-scottsboroboys.

Pilkington, Ed. "Last Three of Scottsboro Nine Receive Posthumous
Pardons for 1931 'Crime.'" *Guardian* (London), Nov. 21, 2013.
theguardian.com/world/2013/nov/21/scottsboro-nine-boys-
posthumous-pardons.

Scottsboro Boys Museum and Cultural Center. scottsboro-multicultural.
com/.

"Scottsboro Boys, Trial and Defense Campaign (1931–1937)."
BlackPast.org. blackpast.org/aah/scottsboro-boys-trial-and-defense-
campaign-1931-1937.

"Scottsboro: An American Tragedy. Who Were the Scottsboro Boys?"
American Experience, 2001. pbs.org/wgbh/americanexperience/features/
scottsboro-boys-who-were-the-boys/.

PLACES TO VISIT

Morgan County Archives
624 Bank Street NE
Decatur, Alabama 35601
(256) 351-4726
co.morgan.al.us/archivesindex.html

Although not a museum, the Morgan County Archives maintains an
exhibit displaying a unique collection of photographs and other items
from the 1933 trial of Haywood Patterson.

Scottsboro Boys Museum and Cultural Center
428 West Willow Street
Scottsboro, Alabama 35768
Phone: (256) 244-1310
scottsboro-multicultural.com

Housed in the former Joyce Chapel United Methodist Church, the museum and cultural center houses collections and exhibits about the nine Scottsboro Boys and also offers educational programs that explore the trials' role in the modern civil rights movement.

Scottsboro Jackson Heritage Center
208 South Houston Street
Scottsboro, Alabama 35768
Phone: (256) 259-2122
sjhc.us

A historical and cultural museum, the heritage center focuses on the history, customs, traditions, and art of Jackson County, and allows visitors to step back in time in its pioneer village.

FURTHER READING

Bartoletti, Susan Campbell. *They Called Themselves the K.K.K.: The Birth of an American Terrorist Group*. Boston: Houghton Mifflin Harcourt, 2010.

Brimner, Larry Dane. *Birmingham Sunday*. Honesdale, PA: Calkins Creek, 2010.

———. *Black and White: The Confrontation between Reverend Fred L. Shuttlesworth and Eugene "Bull" Connor*. Honesdale, PA: Calkins Creek, 2011.

———. *Twelve Days in May: Freedom Ride 1961*. Honesdale, PA: Calkins Creek, 2017.

———. *We Are One: The Story of Bayard Rustin*. Honesdale, PA: Calkins Creek, 2007.

Krull, Kathleen. *A Kids' Guide to America's Bill of Rights*. New York: HarperCollins Children's Books, 2015.

Levinson, Cynthia, and Sanford Levinson. *Fault Lines in the Constitution: The Framers, Their Fights, and the Flaws That Affect Us Today*. Atlanta, GA: Peachtree, 2017.

ACKNOWLEDGMENTS

For unselfishly giving of their time and expertise, my heartfelt thanks to the following: John Allison, archivist, Morgan County Archives; Laura Anderson, Alabama Humanities Foundation; James L. Baggett, archivist, Birmingham Public Library, Department of Archives and Manuscripts; Cathy Bonnell, librarian (retired); Joan Broerman, research assistant and writer; Courtney Pinkard, reference archivist, Alabama Department of Archives and History; Cookie Sharp, assistant director, Scottsboro Jackson Heritage Center; and Shelia Washington, chair, executive committee, Scottsboro Boys Museum and Cultural Center.

SOURCE NOTES

The source of each quotation in this book is found below. The citation indicates the first words of the quotation and its document source. The sources are listed either in the bibliography or below.

FRONT MATTER

"What happened in . . .": Patterson and Conrad, p. 192.

"all persons born . . .": US Constitution, Fourteenth Amendment, Section 1.

Sidebar: Who Were the Scottsboro Boys?

"were riding . . .": Patterson and Conrad, p. 6.

CHAPTER 1: JOURNEY INTERRUPTED

"stealing a ride.": Patterson and Conrad, p. 3.

"with a white . . .": Patterson and Conrad, p. 3.

"hoboing from . . .": Patterson and Conrad, pp. 3–4.

"Some of . . ." and "and some we . . .": Patterson and Conrad, p. 4.

"capture every negro . . .": M. L. Wann, quoted in Carter, p. 5.

"Negroes together": Patterson and Conrad, p. 5.

"Some had not . . ." and "A few in . . .": Patterson and Conrad, p. 6.

"Assault and . . .": unidentified man, quoted in Patterson and Conrad, p. 5.

"two girls . . .": Patterson and Conrad, p. 5.

"flat bars . . .": Patterson and Conrad, p. 6.

"mad ants . . .": Patterson and Conrad, p. 7.

"If you come in . . .": M. L. Wann, quoted in Norris and Washington, p. 21.

"the two gals . . .": Patterson and Conrad, p. 7.

"Miss Price . . .": M. L. Wann, quoted in Norris and Washington, p. 21.

"until she had . . .": Norris and Washington, p. 21.

"Well, if those . . .": unidentified guard, quoted in Norris and Washington, p. 21.

"right hand . . .": Norris and Washington, p. 21.

"You know . . .": unidentified guard, quoted in Norris and Washington, p. 21.

"knew if a . . .": Norris and Washington, p. 22.

CHAPTER 2: ACCUSED

"Only a Negro . . .": Patterson and Conrad, p. 14.

"society was America's . . .": Julian Bond, preface, in Klanwatch Project, *Ku Klux Klan*, p. 5.

"orderly, though it . . .": "How the Nine Arrests at Scottsboro Were Effected," *Huntsville* [AL] *Daily Times*, March 26, 1931.

"jimcrow jail": Patterson and Conrad, p. 6.

"NINE NEGRO MEN . . .": "Nine Negro Men Rape Two White Girls, Charged," *Jackson County* [AL] *Sentinel*, March 26, 1931 (cited as "Nine Negro Men").

"REVOLTING IN . . .": Peter Piper, "Revolting in Last Degree in Story of Girls," *Huntsville* [AL] *Daily Times*, March 26, 1931 (cited as "Revolting in Last Degree").

"one of the most . . .": "Revolting in Last Degree."

"nine negro fiends . . .": "Revolting in Last Degree."

"the details . . .": "National Guard Protects Nine Negroes Held for Assault on White Girls," *Progressive Age* (Scottsboro, AL), March 26, 1931.

"While some of the . . ." and "others of the fiends . . .": "Nine Negro Men."

"Suddenly the 12 . . .": "Revolting in Last Degree."

"onto the ladder . . ." and "the butt end . . ." and "landing so that . . .": "Revolting in Last Degree."

"after a night . . .": "Revolting in Last Degree."

"three companies . . .": "Revolting in Last Degree."

"the worst negro . . .": "Revolting in Last Degree."

"the [two] negros . . .": "Revolting in Last Degree."

"confessed to . . .": "Revolting in Last Degree."

"One of the younger . . .": "Nine Negro Men."

"the negroes would be . . .": "Revolting in Last Degree."

"The general temper . . .": "Negroes Indicted on Charges of Rape," *Jackson County* [AL] *Sentinel*, April 2, 1931.

CHAPTER 3: A HOT TIME IN THE OLD TOWN

"On conviction . . ." and "This was a . . .": "Death Penalty Properly
 Demanded in Fiendish Crime of Nine Burly Negroes," *Huntsville* [AL]
 Daily Times, March 27, 1931.

"doddering . . .": unidentified, quoted in Carter, p. 18.

"unpopular ideas": Carter, p. 18.

"the crowd was . . .": Norris and Washington, p. 22.

"I am here . . .": Stephen R. Roddy, quoted in record of Circuit Court
 of Jackson County, no. 2402, State of Alabama vs. Ozie Powell,
 Willie Roberson, Andy Wright, Olen Montgomery, and Eugene
 Williams, Indictment, filed March 31, 1931, transcript, p. 88, in
 Powell v. Alabama, 287 U.S. 45 (1932), no. 98, Ozie Powell, Willie
 Roberson, Andy Wright and Olen Montgomery, Petitioners, vs. State
 of Alabama (cited as Circuit Court of Jackson County, no. 2402,
 Alabama v. Powell).

"which ones . . .": Norris and Washington, p. 22.

"claim is without . . .": Ibid.

"The evidence against . . .": Ibid.

"took the stand . . .": Norris and Washington, p. 23.

"They said we used . . .": Norris and Washington, p. 23.

"the colored boys . . .": Ruby Bates, quoted in Carter, p. 30.

"I have not . . .": Victoria Price, quoted in record of Circuit Court of
 Jackson County, no. 2404, State of Alabama v. Haywood Patterson,
 Indictment, filed March 31, 1931, transcript, p. 26, in Powell v.
 Alabama, 287 U.S. 45 (1932), no. 99, Haywood Patterson, Petitioner,
 v. State of Alabama (cited as Circuit Court of Jackson County, no.
 2404, Alabama v. Patterson).

"We find . . .": unidentified circuit court clerk, quoted in Carter, p. 37.

"There'll Be . . .": "Patterson v. State, 141 So. 195 (Ala. 1932)," Linder,
 Famous Trials, famous-trials.com/scottsboroboys/1543-patt, accessed
 May 22, 2018.

"standing at the . . .": Ory Dobbins, quoted in Circuit Court of Jackson
 County, no. 2404, Alabama v. Patterson, transcript, p. 34.

"I was not . . .": Haywood Patterson, quoted in Circuit Court of Jackson
 County, no. 2404, Alabama v. Patterson, transcript, p. 38.

"I saw nobody . . .": Patterson and Conrad, p. 12.

"nine negroes . . .": Roy Wright, quoted in Circuit Court of Jackson County, no. 2404, Alabama v. Patterson, transcript, p. 39.

"Five of these . . .": Roy Wright, quoted in Circuit Court of Jackson County, no. 2404, Alabama v. Patterson, transcript, p. 41.

"whipped me . . .": Roy Wright, quoted in F. Raymond Daniell, "Negro Lad Tells Scottsboro Story," *New York Times*, March 10, 1933.

"I was convicted . . .": Patterson and Conrad, p. 13.

"The first one . . .": Price, quoted in Circuit Court of Jackson County, no. 2402, Alabama v. Powell, transcript, p. 22.

"Eugene Williams . . .": Price, quoted in Circuit Court of Jackson County, no. 2402, Alabama v. Powell, transcript, p. 23.

"I didn't testify . . .": Price, quoted in Circuit Court of Jackson County, no. 2402, Alabama v. Powell, transcript, p. 26.

"it took three . . .": Price, quoted in Circuit Court of Jackson County, no. 2402, Alabama v. Powell, transcript, p. 24.

"They all came . . .": Bates, quoted in Circuit Court of Jackson County, no. 2402, Alabama v. Powell, transcript, p. 26.

"My overalls . . .": Bates, quoted in Circuit Court of Jackson County, no. 2402, Alabama v. Powell, transcript, p. 27.

"I did not see no . . .": Ozie Powell, quoted in Circuit Court of Jackson County, no. 2402, Alabama v. Powell, transcript, pp. 33–34.

"I am the boy . . .": Willie Roberson, quoted in Circuit Court of Jackson County, no. 2402, Alabama v. Powell, transcript, pp. 36–37.

"I did not even . . .": Andy Wright, quoted in Circuit Court of Jackson County, no. 2402, Alabama v. Powell, transcript, p. 38.

"I did not have . . .": Olen Montgomery, quoted in Circuit Court of Jackson County, no. 2402, Alabama v. Powell, transcript, p. 39.

"I did not see . . .": Eugene Williams, quoted in Circuit Court of Jackson County, no. 2402, Alabama v. Powell, transcript, p. 41.

"I saw every . . ." and "Yes, sir": Orville Gilley, quoted in Circuit Court of Jackson County, no. 2402, Alabama v. Powell, transcript, pp. 47–48.

"the jury stood . . .": "Eight Negroes Get Death Sentences for Assault on Huntsville White Girls," *Progressive Age* (Scottsboro, AL), April 9, 1931 (cited as "Eight Negroes Get Death").

"Judge Hawkins sentenced . . .": Norris and Washington, p. 24.

"Yes, I have something . . .": Patterson and Conrad, p. 14.

"In Keeping with . . .": Judge Alfred E. Hawkins, quoted in "Eight Negroes Get Death."

"see where . . .": Patterson and Conrad, p. 15.

"Bring me some . . ." and "We're going . . .": Patterson and Conrad, p. 15.

"serious" and "The cell door . . .": Patterson and Conrad, p. 16.

"Negroes Riot . . .": "Negroes Riot in Gadsden to Protest Doom," *Huntsville* [AL] *Daily Times*, April 10, 1931.

CHAPTER 4: A LEGAL LYNCHING

"legally lynch . . ." and "immediate change of . . .": "Judge Threatened by Negro League," *Progressive Age* (Scottsboro, AL), April 9, 1931.

"new trial for . . .": M. C. Walsh, telegram to Governor Miller, dated May 18, 1931.

"immediate safe . . .": Bertha Markowitz, postcard to Governor B. M. Miller, undated.

"The last thing . . .": Carter, pp. 52–53.

"Two guys from . . .": Patterson and Conrad, p. 18.

"You will burn . . .": Claude Patterson, quoted in Carter, p. 58.

"full confidence . . .": letter, quoted in Kinshasa, p. 23.

"advised me that . . ." and "trying to . . ." and "Clarence Norris feels . . .": Powell, quoted in "Condemned Lads Write N.A.A.C.P.," *Pittsburgh Courier*, May 23, 1931.

"There were sixteen . . .": Norris and Washington, p. 48.

"When they turned . . .": Patterson and Conrad, p. 25.

"every single one . . .": Janie Patterson et al., letter to ILD, quoted in Kinshasa, p. 43.

"i want you have . . ." and "Willie Robinson": Roberson, letter to Walter White, quoted in Kinshasa, p. 45.

"It has been . . .": Clarence Norris, letter to White, quoted in Kinshasa, p. 47.

"I learned you . . .": Claude Patterson, letter to White, quoted in Kinshasa, p. 49.

"Mr. Darrow declared . . .": "Darrow Drops Fight to Save Eight Negroes, Refusing to Enter Case with Communists," *New York Times*, December 30, 1931.

"made a written . . .": signed statement, quoted in Kinshasa, p. 68.

"you have chosen . . .": White, letter to Roberson and Weems, quoted in Kinshasa, p. 71.

CHAPTER 5: REPRIEVE

"July came very . . .": Patterson and Conrad, p. 25.

"the case up . . .": Patterson and Conrad, p. 25.

"The forces fighting . . .": "I.L.D. Ask for New Scottsboro Trial," *Press-Forum Weekly* (Mobile, AL), January 30, 1932 (cited as "I.L.D. Ask").

"railroaded . . .": M. C. Walsh, telegram to Governor Miller, dated May 18, 1931.

"Letters and telegrams . . ." and "court would do . . .": Sam Slate, "Knight Seeks Death Penalty for 8 Negroes," *Anniston* [AL] *Star*, January 22, 1932.

"Throughout the trial . . .": George W. Chamlee Sr., quoted ibid.

"mob spirit . . ." and "terrorized the judge . . .": Ibid.

"was convicted . . .": "I.L.D. Ask."

"there is no . . ." and "proceeded to call . . .": "I.L.D. Ask."

"that the speed . . .": "Backs Conviction of Seven Negroes," *New York Times*, March 25, 1932.

"If there were more . . .": opinion written by Thomas E. Knight Sr., quoted ibid.

"The state of Alabama . . .": Knight Sr., quoted ibid.

"was reversed on . . .": "Sentence on 7 Blacks Upheld by High Court," *Anniston* [AL] *Star*, March 24, 1932.

"In justice to . . .": John C. Anderson, quoted in "Counsel Seeks Rehearing for Seven Negroes," *Anniston* [AL] *Star*, March 25, 1932.

"issued a formal . . .": "Ala. Atty. General Tries to Stop Telegrams," *Pittsburgh Courier*, April 16, 1932.

"illegal, libelous . . .": Thomas E. Knight Jr., quoted ibid.

"gross race prejudice . . .": "Germans Protest Doom of Negroes," *Baltimore Sun*, April 16, 1932.

"I have just read . . .": James M. Proctor, letter to the editor, *Manchester* [England] *Guardian*, June 14, 1932.

"The mere fact . . ." and "because of their race . . .": Knight Jr., Brief for Respondent, transcript, p. 32, in Powell v. Alabama, 287 U.S. 45 (1932), nos. 98, 99, 100.

"were not denied . . ." and "by counsel from . . .": Knight Jr., Brief for Respondent, transcript, p. 11, in Powell v. Alabama, 287 U.S. 45 (1932), nos. 98, 99, 100.

"capable counsel . . .": Knight Jr., Brief for Respondent," transcript, p. 13, in Powell v. Alabama, 287 U.S. 45 (1932), nos. 98, 99, 100.

"whether the defendants . . .": "Text of U.S. Supreme Court's Decision in the Scottsboro Case and Dissenting Opinion," the *New York Times*, November 8, 1932.

"From the time . . .": Ibid.

"Negroes of Birmingham . . .": "New Trial Ordered by Supreme Court in Scottsboro Case," *New York Times*, November 8, 1932.

"They made us . . .": Norris and Washington, p. 49.

"came to my . . .": Norris and Washington, p. 50.

"The boys shouted . . .": Patterson and Conrad, p. 34.

CHAPTER 6: A NEW YEAR, A NEW TRIAL

"Over Alabama . . .": Langston Hughes, p. 61.

"I did not . . ." and "So I said . . .": Langston Hughes, p. 61.

"Since the supreme . . .": Montgomery, letter to William L. Patterson, quoted in Kinshasa, p. 81.

"I am . . .": Roy Wright, letter to Patterson, quoted in Kinshasa, p. 92.

"prove beyond question . . .": Carter, p. 181.

"Gentlemen, no matter . . .": Samuel S. Leibowitz, quoted in Robert Leibowitz, *The Defender* (cited as *The Defender*), p. 190.

"You will be . . .": Joseph R. Brodsky, quoted in *The Defender*, p. 190.

"If it is justice . . .": Leibowitz, quoted in *The Defender*, p. 190.

"They got depositions . . .": Norris and Washington, p. 63.

"remaining star . . .": F. Raymond Daniell, "Demands the Chair for Seven Negroes," *New York Times*, March 25, 1933.

"Those police man . . .": Bates, quoted in Carter, pp. 186–87.

"The Decatur jail . . .": Norris and Washington, p. 64.

"on the ground . . .": ." F. Raymond Daniell, "Renew Fight Today in Scottsboro Case," *New York Times*, March 27, 1933.

"The South's . . .": Ibid.

"I know some . . .": J. S. Benson, quoted in F. Raymond Daniell, "Fight for Negroes Opens in Alabama," *New York Times*, March 28, 1933 (cited as "Fight for Negroes").

"They're not trained . . .": Benson, quoted in *The Defender*, p. 199.

"They'll all steal": Benson, quoted in "Fight for Negroes."

"exclusion" and "selection": Knight Jr., quoted in *The Defender*, p. 199; also in "Fight for Negroes."

"the political leaders . . .": Carter, p. 196.

"You are not . . .": Leibowitz, quoted in Carter, p. 198.

"And you don't . . .": Knight Jr., quoted in Carter, p. 198.

"Call him . . .": Leibowitz, quoted in F. Raymond Daniell, "Refuses to Quash Scottsboro Case," *New York Times*, March 29, 1933.

"I'm not . . .": Knight Jr., quoted ibid.

"Now gentlemen . . .": Judge James Edwin Horton Jr., State of Alabama v. Haywood Patterson, Circuit Court of Morgan County, Decatur, AL, March 31, 1933, transcript of testimony (cited as Alabama v. Patterson, Decatur, 1933, transcript).

"twelve minutes . . .": F. Raymond Daniell, "Girl Repeats Story in Scottsboro Case," *New York Times*, April 4, 1933 (cited as "Girl Repeats Story").

"unhesitatingly" and "as one of . . .": "Girl Repeats Story."

"Are those . . ." and "Have they . . ." and "Are they now . . .": Knight Jr., Alabama v. Patterson, Decatur, 1933, transcript.

"This is the first . . .": Leibowitz, Alabama v. Patterson, Decatur, 1933, transcript.

"picked them up . . .": Patterson and Conrad, p. 40.

"not permit . . .": Judge Horton, Alabama v. Patterson, Decatur, 1933, transcript.

"That is a fairly . . .": Leibowitz, Alabama v. Patterson, Decatur, 1933, transcript.

"I won't go by . . .": Price, Alabama v. Patterson, Decatur, 1933, transcript.

"Because that is not . . .": Price, Alabama v. Patterson, Decatur, 1933, transcript.

"Of course you . . .": Leibowitz, Alabama v. Patterson, Decatur, 1933, transcript.

"kinda . . ." and "was bigger . . .": Price, Alabama v. Patterson, Decatur, 1933, transcript.

"certified copies . . .": "Girl Repeats Story."

"had been arrested . . .": "Girl Repeats Story."

"By the way . . .": Leibowitz, Alabama v. Patterson, Decatur, 1933, transcript.

"with a white . . .": F. Raymond Daniell, "Evidence Assailed in Alabama Trial," *New York Times*, April 5, 1933.

"I'm going to show . . .": Leibowitz, quoted ibid.

"the Price woman's . . .": F. Raymond Daniell, "Warning by Judge at Alabama Trial," *New York Times*, April 6, 1933 (cited as "Warning by Judge").

"was sufficient . . .": "Warning by Judge."

"the two women . . .": "Warning by Judge."

"I saw them . . .": Percy Ricks, quoted in "Warning by Judge."

"tried at . . .": Knight Jr., quoted in Patterson and Conrad, p. 42.

"No, sir . . .": Patterson and Conrad, p. 42.

"Who told you . . .": Knight Jr., quoted in Patterson and Conrad, p. 42.

"I told myself . . .": Patterson and Conrad, p. 42.

"that a mob . . .": "Warning by Judge."

"The court wishes . . .": Judge Horton, quoted in "Warning by Judge."

"If these defendants . . .": Judge Horton, quoted in "Warning by Judge."

"may expect to . . .": Judge Horton, quoted in "Warning by Judge."

"Judge Horton left . . .": F. Raymond Daniell, "Girl Recants Story of Negroes' Attack," *New York Times*, April 7, 1933.

"Mrs. Price was . . .": Ibid.

"She came alone . . .": Rev. Dr. Harry Emerson Fosdick, quoted ibid.

"confessional" and "tell the truth": Fosdick, quoted ibid.

"I told it . . .": Bates, quoted ibid.

"to see that . . .": Leibowitz, quoted in F. Raymond Daniell, "New York Attacked in Scottsboro Trial," *New York Times*, April 8, 1933.

"show them . . .": Wade Wright, quoted ibid.

"Don't you know . . .": Wade Wright, quoted ibid.

"You are not trying . . .": Judge Horton, quoted in F. Raymond Daniell, "Jury out Overnight with Scottsboro Case; Judge Warns of Bigotry and Racial Issue," *New York Times*, April 9, 1933.

"The sun came in . . .": Patterson and Conrad, p. 44.

"I am taking . . ." and "But I am . . .": Leibowitz, quoted in F. Raymond Daniell, "Negro Is Convicted in Scottsboro Case," *New York Times*, April 10, 1933 (cited as "Negro Is Convicted").

"an act of . . .": Leibowitz, quoted in "Appeal Brings Same Verdict in Negro Case," *Chicago Tribune*, April, 10, 1933.

"a mockery of . . ." and "a piece of . . .": Leibowitz, quoted in "Negro Is Convicted."

"I ain't had . . .": Patterson, quoted in F. Raymond Daniell, "Scottsboro Case off Indefinitely," *New York Times*, April 18, 1933.

"the passions . . .": Carter, p. 246.

"History, sacred and . . .": Judge Horton, quoted in *The Scottsboro Case: Opinion of Judge James E. Horton* (New York: Scottsboro Defense Committee, January 1936), pp. 25–26; also quoted in part in "Points of Opinion in Scottsboro Case," *New York Times*, June 23, 1933.

"got sore as hell . . .": Patterson and Conrad, p. 49.

CHAPTER 7: BEFORE JUDGE CALLAHAN

"the toughest . . .": Patterson and Conrad, p. 49.

"was a redneck . . .": Norris and Washington, p. 79.

"wanted to get . . .": Norris and Washington, p. 79.

"reporters nicknamed . . .": Norris and Washington, p. 79.

"the jury roll . . .": F. Raymond Daniell, "Ruby Bates Dying; Evidence Sought," *New York Times*, November 25, 1933.

"the honesty of . . .": F. Raymond Daniell, "Jury Roll Upheld in Alabama Case," *New York Times*, November 26, 1933.

"We're going to . . .": Judge William Washington Callahan, quoted in Carter, p. 284.

"the difference between . . .": Judge Callahan, quoted in F. Raymond Daniell, "Accuser Renames Scottsboro Negro," *New York Times*, November 28, 1933 (cited as "Accuser Renames Scottsboro Negro").

"few more flicks . . .": Judge Callahan, quoted in "Accuser Renames Scottsboro Negro."

"I hope you'll . . .": Judge Callahan, quoted in "Accuser Renames Scottsboro Negro."

"hurry it . . ." and "that's enough . . .": Judge Callahan, quoted in Carter, p. 284.

"treat the lady . . .": Judge Callahan, quoted in "Accuser Renames Scottsboro Negro."

"But, your Honor . . .": Leibowitz, quoted in F. Raymond Daniell, "Price Girl's Story Upheld by 'Hobo,'" *New York Times*, November 29, 1933.

"I can imagine": Judge Callahan, quoted ibid.

"disremembered": Patterson, quoted ibid.

"We was scared . . .": Patterson, quoted ibid.

"What do you . . ." and "rotten from . . .": Leibowitz, quoted in F. Raymond Daniell, "Leibowitz Protest Bars 'Confessions,'" *New York Times*, November 30, 1933.

"passion for . . .": Knight Jr., quoted in F. Raymond Daniell, "Scottsboro Case Given to the Jury Which Is Locked Up," *New York Times*, December 1, 1933.

"guarantees . . . a fair, just . . .": Judge Callahan, "Judge Callahan's Charge to the Scottsboro Jury in the Case of Heywood Patterson," *New York Times*, December 1, 1933.

"The law would . . .": Ibid.

"Take the case . . .": Ibid.

"I believe I . . .": Ibid.

"We find . . .": John Green, quoted in F. Raymond Daniell, "Scottsboro Negro Again Condemned," *New York Times*, December 2, 1933.

"noticed he left . . ." and "didn't even . . .": Patterson and Conrad, p. 50.

"A Questionable . . .": F. Raymond Daniell, "Scottsboro Trial Takes New Turn," *New York Times*, December 3, 1933.

"The record of . . .": Ibid.

"He's not guilty . . .": Bates, quoted in F. Raymond Daniell, "Negro's Case Goes to Alabama Jury," *New York Times*, December 5, 1933.

"had been . . .": F. Raymond Daniell, "Scottsboro Negro Is Convicted Again," *New York Times*, December 7, 1933.

"the jury commission": Knight Jr., quoted in "Scottsboro Appeal Raises Jury Issue," *New York Times*, May 26, 1934.

"had not been filed . . .": Carter, p. 307.

"properly rewarded": Carter, p. 309.

"the offer had . . .": "Held as 'Bribers' in Scottsboro Case," *New York Times*, October 2, 1934.

"I knew nothing . . ." and "removed from . . .": Leibowitz, quoted in "Leibowitz Threatens to Quit Negro Case," *New York Times*, October 4, 1934.

"there was a long . . .": Carter, p. 319.

"There is no . . .": Chief Justice Charles Evans Hughes, "Ruling of the Supreme Court in the Scottsboro Cases," *New York Times*, April 2, 1935; also, in Norris v. Alabama, 294 U.S. 587 (1935).

"in the criminal . . .": Ibid.

"the judgment . . .": Ibid.

"the state court . . .": Patterson v. Alabama, 294 U.S. 600 (1935).

"new devices . . .": John Temple Graves, "Scottsboro Ruling Disturbs the South," *New York Times*, April 7, 1935.

"Many Alabamians . . .": Ibid.

"veteran harlot . . ." and "a mockery of . . .": Leibowitz, quoted in Carter, p. 328.

"Subversive elements . . .": Leibowitz, quoted in "Scottsboro Pardons Asked by Leibowitz," *New York Times*, May 1, 1935.

"swore to nine . . .": "New Warrants Sworn for Scottsboro Trial," *New York Times*, May 2, 1935.

"We had been . . .": Norris and Washington, p. 147.

CHAPTER 8: A FAIR TRIAL

"around the country . . .": Patterson and Conrad, p. 61.

"chairman of . . .": "New Indictments in Scottsboro Case with Negro on Jury," *New York Times*, November 14, 1935.

"I don't know . . ." and "I have often . . .": Norris and Washington, p. 148.

"They were afraid . . .": Patterson and Conrad, p. 62.

"immaterial": Judge Callahan, quoted in F. Raymond Daniell, "Scottsboro Judge Is Accused of Bias," *New York Times*, January 22, 1936 (cited as "Scottsboro Judge Is Accused").

"That strikes me . . .": Judge Callahan, quoted in "Scottsboro Judge Is Accused."

"to minimize the . . .": Clarence Watts, quoted in "Scottsboro Judge Is Accused."

"sizzling mad": "Scottsboro Judge Is Accused."

"Don't go out . . .": Melvin C. Hutson, quoted in F. Raymond Daniell, "Scottsboro Case Goes to the Jury," *New York Times*, January 23, 1936.

"It takes courage . . .": Watts, quoted ibid.

"they must assume . . .": Callahan, quoted ibid.

"fixed his punishment . . .": F. Raymond Daniell, "75 Years in Prison Set for Patterson," *New York Times*, January 24, 1936.

"I'd rather die . . .": Patterson, quoted ibid.

"'Twant fair": Price, quoted ibid.

"He was never . . .": Norris and Washington, p. 166.

"the three manacled . . .": F. Raymond Daniell, "Scottsboro Negro Shot Trying Break as He Stabs Guard," *New York Times*, January 25, 1936.

"come out . . ." and "Blalock wheeled . . .": Norris and Washington, pp. 162–63.

"These sons of . . .": Edgar Blalock, quoted in Norris and Washington, p. 163.

"I am going . . .": J. Street Sandlin, quoted in Norris and Washington, p. 163.

CHAPTER 9: HALF OUT AND HALF IN

"A child would . . .": Norris and Washington, p. 169.

"her reputation . . .": F. Raymond Daniell, "Scottsboro Trial Rushed to Finish," *New York Times*, July 15, 1937.

"I would not . . .": F. Raymond Daniell, "Scottsboro Trial Rushed to Finish," *New York Times*, July 15, 1937.

"Two of the Negroes . . .": Hutson, quoted in F. Raymond Daniell, "Tries to Speed Up Scottsboro Cases," *New York Times*, July 19, 1937.

"One never can . . .": Hutson, quoted ibid.

"It seems to . . .": Leibowitz, quoted in F. Raymond Daniell, "Scottsboro Trial Drops Death Plea," *New York Times*, July 20, 1937.

"I can't fight . . .": Leibowitz, quoted in F. Raymond Daniell, "Scottsboro Jury Asked to Give Life," *New York Times*, July 21, 1937.

"knockout punch": Leibowitz, quoted ibid.

"I ain't got . . .": Andy Wright, quoted in F. Raymond Daniell, "Scottsboro Jurors Give 99-Year Term," *New York Times*, July 22, 1937.

"It is not . . .": Judge Callahan, quoted in F. Raymond Daniell, "Scottsboro Judge Warns Leibowitz," *New York Times*, July 23, 1937.

"I move that . . .": Leibowitz, quoted ibid.

"trained seals . . ." and "performers . . .": Leibowitz, quoted in F. Raymond Daniell, "Weems Case Given to Alabama Jury," *New York Times*, July 24, 1937.

"poppycock": Leibowitz, quoted ibid.

"I'm sick . . .": Leibowitz, quoted ibid.

"I'm guilty . . .": Powell, quoted in F. Raymond Daniell, "Scottsboro Case Ends as 4 Go Free: 2 More Get Prison," *New York Times*, July 25, 1937 (cited as "Scottsboro Case Ends").

"Neither the Sheriff . . .": "Scottsboro Case Ends."

"with their hands . . .": "Scottsboro Case Ends."

"Gee, I haven't . . .": unidentified Scottsboro defendant, quoted in "Scottsboro Case Ends"; identified as Montgomery in Goodman, p. 337.

"It was the . . .": Norris and Washington, p. 171.

"For the boys . . .": Patterson and Conrad, p. 68.

"a case of . . .": "Scottsboro Case Ends."

"If five of . . .": Norris and Washington, p. 171.

"Weren't we either . . .": Norris and Washington, p. 171.

"either all were . . .": Carter, p. 377.

"It is nothing . . .": Leibowitz, quoted in "Scottsboro Case Ends."

"I knew I . . .": Patterson and Conrad, p. 68.

"I cannot make . . .": Governor Bibb Graves, quoted in Carter, p. 381.

"court affirmed . . .": "Court Affirms Sentences of 2 in Scottsboro Case," *Morning Call* (Allentown, PA), June 10, 1938.

"Dr. Chalmers was . . .": Norris and Washington, p. 173.

"Please defer . . .": Governor Bibb Graves, quoted in Carter, p. 389.

"Governor Graves denied . . .": "Scottsboro Rape Case Convicts Denied Pardons," *Enterprise-Journal* (McComb, MS), November 15, 1938.

"refused to pardon . . .": Norris and Washington, p. 174.

"He reneged . . .": Norris and Washington, pp. 174–75.

"settled into . . .": Norris and Washington, p. 175.

"The people all . . .": Patterson and Conrad, p. 69.

CHAPTER 10: OBSCURITY

"The damage which . . .": Roy Wilkins, letter to Eugene Martin, Atlanta Life Insurance Company, quoted in Kinshasa, p. 234.

"suffered sufficiently": "Alabama's New Board of Pardons Gets Plea of Much-Disputed Scottsboro Rape Case," *Corpus Christi* [TX] *Caller-Times*, January 19, 1940.

"the most ticklish . . .": Ibid.

"a day for . . .": Alex Smith, quoted in "Parole Denied to 5 in Scottsboro Case," *New York Times*, March 9, 1940.

"A guard attacked . . .": Norris and Washington, p. 181.

"free streets" and "It might as well . . .": Norris and Washington, p. 193.

"Andy and me . . .": Norris and Washington, p. 195.

"I had been . . .": Norris and Washington, p. 200.

"My name is . . .": Norris and Washington, p. 209.

"They tell me . . .": Chalmers, quoted in Patterson and Conrad, p. 228.

"No damn record . . .": Patterson and Conrad, p. 229.

"I am giving . . .": Patterson and Conrad, p. 229.

"Prison Director Frank Boswell . . .": "Scottsboro Case Prisoner Escapes," *Tucson* [AZ] *Daily Citizen*, July 21, 1948.

"I began to . . ." and "right down in . . .": Patterson and Conrad, p. 231.

"I believe I . . .": Andy Wright, quoted in "Last of Famed Scottsboro Rape Case Defendants Still in Prison Ordered Freed," *Palladium-Item* (Richmond, IN), June 7, 1950.

"I've got no . . .": Andy Wright, quoted in "Andy Wright Released from Kilby Prison Here," *Montgomery* [AL] *Advertiser*, June 10, 1950.

CHAPTER 11: BACK IN THE HEADLINES

"left her home . . .": "Ruby Bates Says Show Shattered Her Privacy," *Anniston* [AL] *Star*, May 12, 1976.

"I wish . . .": Bates, quoted ibid.

"I think it . . .": Bates, quoted ibid.

"by suggesting she . . .": "Network Wins 'Scottsboro' Suit," *Herald-Palladium* (Saint Joseph, MI), July 13, 1977 (cited as "Network Wins").

"I could have . . .": Price, quoted in Fred Barbash, "The Real 'Scottsboro' Victim? Victoria Street Could Be One," *Atlanta* [GA] *Constitution*, January 10, 1982.

"There is no . . .": Judge Charles Neese, quoted in "Network Wins."

"I was tired . . .": Norris, quoted in Thomas A. Johnson, "Scottsboro Defendant Applies for a Pardon," *New York Times*, October 9, 1976.

"Fifteen years is . . .": Norris, quoted ibid.

"In my opinion . . .": William J. Baxley, quoted ibid.

"While no act . . .": Nathaniel Jones, quoted in Thomas A. Johnson, "Last of Scottsboro 9 Is Pardoned; He Draws a Lesson for Everybody," *New York Times*, October 26, 1976.

"an old, thin . . .": Shelia Washington, quoted in Matthew Teague, "In Alabama, a Measure of Justice for the Scottsboro Boys," *Los Angeles Times*, November 21, 2013 (cited as "In Alabama, a Measure of Justice").

"You don't need . . ." and "Just keep quiet . . .": "In Alabama, a Measure of Justice."

"We need to . . .": Governor Robert Bentley, quoted in Danielle Wallingsford, "Scottsboro Boys Exonerated," *Clarion* (Scottsboro, AL), April 23, 2013, scottsboro-multicultural.com/articles/Scottsboro%20 Boys%20Exonerated%20%28The%20Clarion%20-%20April%20

23%202013%29.pdf, accessed May 19, 2018 (cited as "Scottsboro Boys Exonerated").

"Today is a . . .": AL state senator Arthur Orr, quoted in Alan Blinder, "Alabama Pardons 3 'Scottsboro Boys' after 80 Years," *New York Times*, November 21, 2013.

"a significant milestone . . .": Orr, quoted ibid.

"We cannot take . . .": Bentley, quoted in "Scottsboro Boys Exonerated."

INDEX

Page numbers in **boldface** refer to images and/or captions.

M

PICTURE CREDITS

Strike! The Farm Workers' Fight for Their Rights

Notable Books for a Global Society Book Award
Orbis Pictus Award Recommended Book
VOYA's Perfect 10
★*Booklist*, STARRED REVIEW
★*Kirkus Reviews*, STARRED REVIEW
★*School Library Journal*, STARRED REVIEW

Twelve Days in May: Freedom Ride 1961

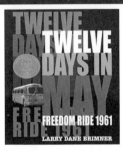

Sibert Medal Winner
Carter G. Woodson Book Award
Booklist Editors' Choice
A Chicago Public Library Best of the Best Book
★*Booklist*, STARRED REVIEW
★*School Library Journal*, STARRED REVIEW

We Are One: The Story of Bayard Rustin

Jane Addams Book Award for Older Children
Norman A. Sugarman Children's Biography Award
New York Public Library Books for the Teen Age
★*School Library Connection*, STARRED REVIEW
★*School Library Journal*, STARRED REVIEW